# Ashley Jackson

Earth to Earth. Pathway to Life.

# Ashley Jackson

## AN ARTIST'S LIFE

Chris Bond

First published in Great Britain in 2010 by
**Wharncliffe Books**
An imprint of
Pen & Sword Books Ltd
47 Church Street
Barnsley
South Yorkshire
S70 2AS

ISBN 978 1 84563 104 8

A CIP catalogue record for this book is
available from the British Library

Printed and bound in Thailand
By Kyodo Nation Printing Services

Pen & Sword Books Ltd incorporates the Imprints of
Pen & Sword Aviation, Pen & Sword Family History, Pen & Sword Maritime,
Pen & Sword Military, Wharncliffe Local History, Pen & Sword Select, Pen & Sword Military Classics,
Leo Cooper, Remember When, Seaforth Publishing and Frontline Publishing

For a complete list of Pen & Sword titles please contact
PEN & SWORD BOOKS LIMITED
47 Church Street, Barnsley, South Yorkshire, S70 2AS, England
E-mail: enquiries@pen-and-sword.co.uk
Website: www.pen-and-sword.co.uk

# Contents

# Acknowledgements

Tate Modern, the Royal Institute of Painters in Watercolours, the Royal Watercolour Society, the Laing Art Gallery, Yorkshire Post Newspapers, Claudia Berettoni, Anne Jackson, Ron Darwent, Ian McMillan, Graham Ibbeson, Tony Christie, Sir Patrick Duffy, Kate Bond, Secker and Warburg, publishers of My Brush with Fortune, Dennis Thorpe, Yorkshire Bank, Faber and Faber Ltd, The Lowry, Marie Parkinson and Lisa Hoosan.

Painting is a strange business
JMW Turner

# Pay Nowt to Come In

For any aspiring young watercolour artist hoping to make a name for themselves, the mid-1960s were perhaps not the best time to start. Although watercolour painting had a long and venerable tradition that pre-dated the Renaissance, and included the likes of Girtin, Turner and Cezanne, as well as such notable twentieth century artists as Kandinsky and Klee among its past practitioners, it was seen as old-fashioned and out of step with the new artistic order that was emerging. In New York, Andy Warhol's subversive pop art creations were already changing preconceived ideas about what art could be. So, too, were Roy Lichtenstein's 'industrial' paintings, which owed more to Mickey Mouse than Michelangelo in terms of inspiration. In Britain, following the post-war years of austerity, the seeds of cultural change were also beginning to bloom. The psychedelic colours of London's Carnaby Street boutiques were reflected in pop works created by talented young artists such as Richard Hamilton, Peter Blake and David Hockney. At the same time, conceptual art was quickly gaining kudos with Gilbert & George and Keith Arnatt among its leading exponents. Times were changing and with the sixties starting to swing to a different beat there seemed little chance for an eager, young watercolourist to

make a living. It was harder still to attempt this in Barnsley, which even its most ardent supporters wouldn't describe as a cultural Mecca. Yet it was against this unpromising backdrop that Ashley Jackson set out to become an artist.

Having quit his full-time signwriting job at the end of 1964 he spent much of the following year scratching around for work. He continued doing the odd bit of signwriting, everything from solicitors' windows to names on coffin plates, but the only money he got from his art came through occasional, and usually uninspiring, commissions or requests to paint people's pets. Ashley and his wife, Anne, had recently moved to Dodworth, which was then still a mining village west of Barnsley. They paid seventeen shillings a week rent for a two-up, two-down, terraced house with a shared outside toilet in a place known locally as 'Top of Dodworth Bottom'. He didn't have a studio at this time and had to work out of the family kitchen, which was hardly ideal. Although Anne worked as a chief clerk for a local insurance firm, they had lost the security that his full-time income gave them:

We jumped in feet first. It was very hard in the beginning because we had no idea whether or not I was going to be able to make a living out of selling my paintings, so there was a lot of pressure on me.

Their social life consisted of little more than weekend walking trips with friends. There were no meals out, no parties and there certainly weren't any holidays.

Although Ashley was now in his mid-twenties and had been painting since his teens, he had only sold a handful of works and the most anyone had paid for one was a mere fifteen shillings (75p in new money). What he needed was the opportunity to show people what he could do, or a bit of luck. One of his favourite paintings was of a derelict cottage called *Ewden Valley*,

A receipt for the sale of an early Ashley Jackson painting.

which he had finished a couple of years earlier. Its mood was darker and more unsettling than the others. He decided to get it framed and took it to a local art shop in Barnsley. He had known the owner Mary Hayden since his days at art college when he bought cheap brushes and paper. She had always encouraged him but Ashley remembers she was taken aback when he showed her this particular painting:

She took it up to the light and said, 'Wow, have you done that?' She told me there was a critics meeting at the Barnsley Art Society the following week and said I should go with her and bring the painting.

Despite the fact that Ashley wasn't a member of the art society she was able to smuggle him in and put his painting on the wall. His was one of 300 works on display, all done by local amateurs. Three professional artists had been invited along as critics and each had to select their favourite painting and discuss its merits.

Everyone had to put tape over their name so the critics couldn't see them and we sat there and waited to see what they thought. I couldn't believe it when two of them chose mine. They praised it to the hilt and then one of them said, 'Will the person who painted this please stand up.' I remember I was sitting next to Miss Hayden and as I stood up I got some dark looks from a few people because I wasn't a member.

Ashley Jackson, Yorkshire Artist

A photo of Ashley from a Yorkshire Bank Leaflet.

Suitably encouraged by the critics' remarks he dedicated as much time as he could to his painting, rifling through old sketchbooks to pick out those that might help improve his technique. Every spare weekend, come rain or shine, he traipsed across the wind-swept Pennines armed with his sketchpads. He slowly built up his portfolio, joined the Barnsley Art Society and began getting mentioned in the local newspapers. They seemed intrigued by the idea of a struggling young artist who specialized in painting the Yorkshire hills. With his fledgling art career appearing to be moving forward, if not yet upward, he sent a selection of paintings to an exhibition of members' works at the art society. But if he was hoping for an enthusiastic reception when he turned up for a meeting he was in for a shock. He had barely walked into the room when one leading member of the society stormed over and branded him an 'imposter', which instantly halted the buzz of conversation. Too stunned to defend himself against the accusation he simply turned round and walked out. He was devastated, but worse was to come. He wrote to the head of the nearby Cooper Art Gallery asking if he could exhibit some of his works there, only to receive a terse reply:

> They wrote back to say the gallery wasn't there to promote local artists and that my work was far too inferior for their gallery. I still have the letter and I remember it whenever I see a young artist who needs encouragement.

It was another blow to the young artist's confidence and for a brief moment he considered quitting and returning to full-time signwriting. But stung by his treatment at the hands of some members of Barnsley's art establishment and with the unwavering support of his wife, he stuck at it. What he needed was to somehow get his work on public display, but as 1964 gave way to a new year, this appeared as illusive as ever. Then, just as every door seemed to be slamming shut, opportunity came knocking in the unlikeliest of places.

A West Yorkshire businessman called Ron Mears had heard about Ashley's work and invited him to display some of his paintings at a soirée to raise funds for the Brighouse branch of the Liberal Party. It wasn't a gallery exhibition, but at least it was a start:

> They asked for ten per cent of any sales, but I would have agreed to ninety because I had to find out if people would actually buy my paintings. So I went along to this wine and cheese evening and took a dozen of my works and sold half of them.

Although the most he got for one of his watercolours was four guineas (£4.40 in modern money), it was better than he had dared hope. The local Liberal Association was also impressed, having made a tidy profit, and realising there was the potential for money to be made out of all this, invited him to hold a full-scale exhibition at their headquarters, a handsome building on Bethel Street, a couple of weeks later.

> That was my first breakthrough, in Brighouse of all places. It was a Saturday morning and I put a notice up saying, 'Ashley Jackson Watercolours Exhibition – pay nowt to come in'.

It did the trick as more than 200 people turned up and out of the twenty paintings on view he sold a dozen, with a further nine people giving him commissions:

> I was gobsmacked because this was the first time I'd been paid more than a pound for a painting. James Pickles the

famous judge was there, and he bought the most expensive one I had for five quid.

Delighted by the exhibition's success, he rang round all the local newspapers he could think of to see if they wanted to run a story about the local artist who'd come good, and several did. Although he wasn't famous and couldn't claim to have painted a masterpiece, his determination had paid off and now he knew, for perhaps the first time in his life, that he could make it as an artist.

Ashley sketching in his early days.

Wainstalls, near Halifax.

# 2

# *Born at the Wrong Time*

Ashley Norman Jackson emerged into a troubled world on October 22, 1940, in the American Hospital, Penang. It was a seemingly incongruous beginning for someone who would later become synonymous with the Yorkshire landscape, but one that was perhaps in keeping with his exotic roots.

Both his father, Norman Valentine Jackson, and his mother Dulcie Olga Scott, were born in Malaya. Dulcie was brought up in the bristling heat of Penang, where her family enjoyed the privileged life afforded them by their British colonial connections. Her father, Captain Cecil Scott, was a Scottish army bandmaster who married a Portuguese girl and remained in the Far East after retiring from the forces. His army pension together with his savings would have given him a modest life back in Britain, but in Penang it meant he and his family could inhabit a luxurious world that included servants, sipping gin tonics in the shade of the veranda and membership of exclusive clubs. Dulcie met her future husband during a family holiday to Singapore, which dwarfed even Penang's considerable opulence. Ashley's grandmother had settled in the city establishing herself as a successful businesswoman, owning a local bus service and a small publishing house. Because the Jacksons and the Scotts were of a similar social standing, it was inevitable that the two families would meet in such a small expat community, where the world revolved around the famous Raffles bar. So as the

Ashley with his mother Dulcie, next to his cousin Priscilla and her mother, Eddie, in India.

elders sipped their gin slings, shared gossip and expressed their concern at the darkening skies gathering over Europe, Norman and Dulcie fell in love. By the time the fortnight's holiday was over and the two families were saying their farewells, the young couple were engaged, although it was another six months before they would meet again – at their wedding in Penang.

Not surprisingly, given both families' social status, the wedding was a lavish affair and the couple honeymooned in the Cameron Highlands before starting their new life together in a family-owned home in Penang. Dulcie was just seventeen years old and Norman, who was ten years older, was very much the man of the house. He inherited his mother's business acumen and worked his way up to become general manager of the Tiger Beer Company in Singapore.

A few years earlier he found himself embroiled in allegations of espionage when the Japanese accused him of working for British Intelligence. Although the evidence remains inconclusive, what is known is that he was friends with a Japanese man living in Singapore and that the pair were arrested and interrogated during a visit to Japan before eventually being released. At the time it seemed unimportant but the incident was to have grave consequences later.

When war broke out in 1939 Norman enlisted in the Singapore Volunteer Reserve. However, while Britain suffered a shortage of food and was being pounded by the Luftwaffe, life in Singapore hadn't changed much. Raffles was as crowded as ever, there was no rationing, no bombs and little to worry about. All that changed with the Japanese attack on the US fleet at Pearl Harbour. Suddenly a war that had, up to that point, been a distant one was now much closer to home. Singapore was

Ashley's parents Norman Jackson and Dulcie Scott on their wedding day.

considered a vital part of the British Empire and seen by many as the 'Gibraltar in the Far East'. As a result it was well defended, with huge guns pointing out to sea and surrounded on three sides by dense jungle. It was, the British military top brass believed, an impregnable fortress. But Norman Jackson didn't share their optimism and by the start of 1942 he was already making plans to get his family out. He shipped his two younger brothers to the safety of the United States and then painstakingly arranged berths for his remaining relatives on different ships out of Singapore, including his young wife and eighteen-month-old son, Ashley.

His concerns proved well founded. In February 1942, the Japanese Army swarmed through the supposedly 'impenetrable' jungle, effectively walking in through the back door. Around 100,000 British and Allied troops surrendered, many of who had only recently arrived to boost the defences, in what Winston Churchill later called 'Britain's greatest defeat' of the war. Singapore fell so swiftly that the Scotts and the Jacksons nearly didn't make it. The Japanese bombarded the fleeing vessels as they steamed out of the harbour, and as the bombs rained down numerous ships were sunk and many lives were lost, including friends of the two families. But the ships carrying Ashley and his family survived this deadly gauntlet and escaped into the relative safety of the Indian Ocean.

However, life on board ship was far from comfortable. The wives and children of army officers were given what few cabins were available while the rest were left to grab what space they could find. And since Ashley's father was only a volunteer, he had no rank, which meant Ashley and his mother had to live and sleep on an open deck. For a young teenage mother used to having servants at her beck and call it was a cold and frightening

Ashley's paternal grandmother.

Ashley's father and grandmother in Malaya before the war.

Ashley's paintings of Penang part of his 1995 exhibition Here's to You Dad.

experience. There was also the agony of being separated from her husband, for he, along with Ashley's grandfather Scott and three uncles, Tommy, Ossie and Leslie, had stayed behind to fight.

Amid all the confusion during the desperate escape from Singapore it became a lottery where families ended up. Some ships headed to Australia, others to India. As luck would have it Ashley's family ended up in Bombay, along with tens of thousands of other refugees. However, the arrival of this frightened, ill-assorted and disorganized mob of women and children meant yet more chaos and uncertainty. Ashley and his mother were left milling around on the docks with crowds of equally frantic women and howling kids until, by chance, they bumped into his Grandma Scott, who had arrived on another ship. After a tearful reunion she took them under her wing and they joined the rest of the family before being sent to a clearance camp on the outskirts of the city. The two grandmothers took charge, using their families' military connections to ensure they were well treated. Arrangements were quickly made for the twelve of them to travel to Bangalore, in the southern Indian state of Karnataka, where they moved into a bungalow in the city's European quarter.

Despite the recent traumatic upheaval they quickly fell into a routine. Two of Ashley's aunts had young children and his uncles, Clive and Sonny Boy, were also with them. They soon found out that most of their old privileges could still be enjoyed as they had been in Penang and Singapore. The one key difference was that the old European class divisions no longer mattered, because whatever army or diplomatic connections people had everyone now felt threatened. This air of despondency deepened with every fresh dispatch, which brought news that the Japanese were driving ever closer to the Indian border.

On the Moor, Wharfedale.

The family members carried on as best they could, keeping their worst fears to themselves. Certainly the sudden arrival of a group of vivacious, young women didn't go unnoticed among the troops stationed in Bangalore and it wasn't long before a string of young officers began appearing at the house offering invitations to regimental balls and cocktail parties. They knew that most of the women were happily married and this was respected, but even escorting one of them to a dance, or the races, would have been a feather in the regimental cap of any officer.

Within a few months the fear that followed their arrival slowly disappeared as the house echoed to the sound of laughter and music. Ashley's Grandma Scott was an accomplished pianist and his aunts became well known for their impression of the Andrews sisters, so much so that they were invited to sing on the all-India radio network. Had they been aware of what was happening to their sons and husbands, though, they wouldn't have been so frivolous. Following Singapore's capitulation they knew they had become Japanese prisoners and taken to Changi Prison. But the women had taken comfort from the fact that the men weren't fighting on the front line and assumed they were safe. The few letters that did find their way to India were heavily censored. There was no hint of the atrocities being committed in the POW camps and no information about the forced labour used to build the infamous jungle railways. The full scale of these horrors was yet to come.

The only person who was causing concern among the family, was Ashley. Compared to Penang and Singapore, he found the oppressive heat of Bangalore unbearable. He suffered several fits and blackouts during the first twelve months in India and even lost his sight for a couple of days, after a particularly severe bout. The doctors and consultants believed he would grow out of his condition, but it persisted. On one occasion he suffered a massive convulsion and swallowed his tongue and was saved only by his grandmother's quick thinking. Grabbing a spoon, she hauled him up by his feet and hung him upside down. She then passed him to his mother and spooned his tongue out with one hand and thumped him on the back with the other. In the months following this drama he gradually grew stronger and by the time he approached his fourth birthday he was starting to explore his surroundings:

I would wander into the servants' houses, even though I wasn't supposed to. I remember the floors of their huts were made from sun-baked cow dung and I would sit cross-legged with the Indian kids.

He picked up bits of the language and joined in their games:

A letter sent by Ashley's father to his family from the concentration camp he later died in.

We went out into the jungle, well it was scrubland really, but it felt like a real jungle to a young boy like me playing Mowgli. There may not have been any Bengal tigers lurking around, but there was the occasional snake and plenty of 'bandy goats' – these huge rats which we were told had been known to attack humans.

Although the war still raged to the east, the Japanese threat had subsided and life became increasingly relaxed. When the scorching summer heat became too much the family joined the temporary exodus up towards the cooler air of the foothills of the outer Himalayas. They bought their own summer house in Nainital where they spent the next couple of summers. The family had a steady stream of cash coming in through army service pensions, which paid for trips to places like Delhi, Bombay and Ceylon. It also allowed them to hire a welter of servants including a cook, maids, *dhobi wallahs* to do the laundry and an *amah*, or nanny, for each child. When Ashley reached his fourth birthday the family threw a special party to celebrate. It was organized by aunt Cissie, his mother's elder sister, and the highlight was the unexpected arrival of a bear charmer:

> There was an elderly, bearded Sikh wearing a floppy turban who had the bear firmly attached to a rope. My mother and aunts laughed as we all ran squealing towards the house.

The bear charmer had been arranged as a special treat. Using a flute-like instrument the man got the bear to dance, albeit ponderously on its hind legs, and was even able to make it do somersaults on the sun-parched ground. Such antics sound

Ashley and his cousins, Evelyn, Leslie and Priscilla, at his memorable fourth birthday, in Bangalore, India.

shocking to us today, but for the young children watching it was a magical sight:

> I'd seen glimpses of snake charmers on street corners and even one who had a cobra and a mongoose, but nothing as spectacular as this.

However, their gentle idyll was about to shatter. Having reached military age, Sonny Boy left to become a Chindit with General Wingate's Fourteenth Army. At the same time news was slowly filtering through to expat families about the horrific maltreatment of prisoners by the Japanese. Despite strict censorship, many letters were hinting at their desperate situation and the ravaging effects of diseases like malaria and dysentery. The news became increasingly bleak. First, the family were told that Sonny Boy had been captured – they found out later that he had been forced to work on the infamous Burma Railway, which claimed the lives of around 16,000 Allied POWs, including Ashley's uncle Leslie Larker. It emerged, too, that Ashley's grandfather Scott and his uncle Tommy Scott were among the slave labourers. However, his father wasn't, although his situation had become even more perilous. Having apparently made several failed attempts to escape he was taken to a secure camp in Borneo, which had a reputation as being the Oriental Colditz. With the Japanese forces now retreating eastwards Allied survivors began emerging out of the jungle, including Sonny Boy. Ashley's grandfather and uncle were also alive, although beaten and badly malnourished. Family members received letters confirming what they had only dared dream, but their celebrations were cut short when news arrived that Ashley's father was missing, presumed dead. Any hope that there may have been a mistake disappeared as the grim facts about his fate slowly emerged. As Australian soldiers closed in on the camp, the guards gave the remaining twenty-six prisoners a shovel and ordered them to dig their own graves. Each was then shot dead. According to some reports, the prisoners were executed just twenty-four hours before the Allies reached the camp. It would be another thirty years before Roy Mason, then Minister of Defence, took up the matter with the War Graves Commission which traced records of the incident and a proper commemoration was added to the cenotaph.

But as the war drew to a close and other families celebrated the safe return of their loved ones, Ashley, who wasn't even five years old, faced an uncertain future. His mother, herself barely in her twenties, was so grief-stricken that relatives even considered adopting Ashley and raising him in India. They reasoned, understandably perhaps, that she would eventually remarry and want to start a new family. Dulcie, though, refused

Ashley looks through old records of his father.

to entertain the idea. Nevertheless, the family unit which had supported one another through the war was beginning to break up. Ashley's grieving grandmother struggled to come to terms with her son's death so when Raul, one of her younger sons who had been sent to America, married and moved to Limerick, she travelled to Ireland to live with him, leaving behind a confused and tearful grandson.

# 3

# There's No Place Called Home

It wasn't long before Ashley also said goodbye to India, the land of his childhood. His grandfather Scott, having recovered sufficiently from his wartime ordeal, decided it was time they moved. He was born in Scotland and it seemed to make sense to return to his homeland, so he arranged for the remaining eight family members to travel to Glasgow. It wasn't a particularly happy time for Ashley and his relatives, who were leaving behind a country they had grown fond of to head into uncharted waters.

The journey to Britain was long, and painfully slow, although it was a welcome contrast to the conditions they were forced to endure when they fled Singapore three years earlier. The boat they travelled on was a luxury liner converted into a troop ship and they had cabins, rather than being left to brave the elements on deck. It was another eight weeks before they finally caught a glimpse of Britain's grey shores through the murk, as they inched towards the mouth of the River Clyde. This was a turbulent time for the family who had mixed emotions as they landed at the docks:

I don't think anyone knew exactly what was going to

Glencoe, Scotland.

happen. Everyone was still recovering from the shock of my father's death and now we were war refugees who had to fend for ourselves.

It's hard to imagine what the adults must have been thinking as they trundled across Glasgow to their new, temporary home – a former army camp at Bridge of Weir, near Paisley. Compared to their life in Bangalore it must have been a miserable existence. Their living quarters consisted of a draughty hut with a corrugated iron roof, which they shared with a group of fellow refugees. There was precious little privacy and even less comfort. The only heat came from a solitary stove in the middle of the hut and if they wanted any water they had to queue up with a bucket in a nearby dining hall. Winter came as a particular shock, especially as they were used to the sweltering heat and humidity of southern India. It wasn't only the climate that was different. While the smell of damp heather and peat moor wasn't unpleasant, the stench of petrol fumes from Glasgow's buses and lorries was a far cry from the soft, scented aromas of Bangalore.

Ashley's grandfather Scott was the only one of the family with any work to do. He travelled to Edinburgh and London where he bought musical instruments and looked up old contacts in an attempt to re-organize the band he ran before the war. The women tried to fit in with their new surroundings and started going to the Saturday night dance, although Glasgow's Mecca Ballroom was a little different from the social whirl they were accustomed to. Ashley and his uncle Clive were sent to school, although they rarely made it to lessons. Their parents, though, were none-the-wiser because there was little or no communication between the school and

Ashley's grandfather Cecil Scott.

the camp. Instead of learning maths and English the two boys made a beeline for the river. It was here that Ashley first started drawing:

> Clive and some of the other children went fishing or made rafts, but I used my schoolbooks as sketchpads and tried to draw the river and the trees and hills in the distance. I remember on my birthday I asked for a paintbox so I could colour in my sketches, but I've got no idea where this came from because it wasn't something I copied off anyone and I didn't get any encouragement.

As time wore on they grew to appreciate the stunning Scottish landscape. The family outings to Loch Lomond and the Highlands where storm clouds raged over the mountains fascinated the boys, particularly Ashley. But if life was slowly improving, his education wasn't. The infrequent appearances at school meant he often ended up at the bottom of the class. However, it wasn't long before his grandfather announced that the family was heading back to Malaya. After nearly two years it was clear that the adults at least weren't going to adapt to the spartan life of post-war Britain and in the autumn of 1947 they headed back home.

The voyage back to South East Asia was a joyous one. They were surrounded by many expat families intent on returning to their old lives, and those on board were in high spirits. When they landed in Penang they were in a state of euphoria, revelling in the warm sunshine and glad to eat the exotic foods and fruits again, instead of the porridge, boiled beef and stewed cabbage of the refugee camp. The family found grandfather Scott's old residence overrun with lizards, but still intact. But when they reached Singapore their elation quickly disappeared. Both the family houses had been razed to the ground, although it was the horrific fate of their servants that appalled them most. The Japanese had tortured and killed many of the Chinese community in Malaya. Some of the victims were filled with water and then stamped on until their bodies burst. Such sickening tales were a reminder to the family of their own losses and their hopes were further dashed when they discovered that the companies in which they had shares had all closed down, leaving Ashley's mother with just her husband's pension to survive on.

The family was held together during these difficult times by Ashley's grandfather Scott, an affable, if eccentric, character. When the weather became too hot he had a huge tent pitched on the lawn into which he moved his bed, furniture, carpets, library and his musical instruments, including a set of bagpipes. Many sultry evenings would be filled with the mournful wail of the Highlands drifting from his tent. He encouraged the women to find work and when Ashley's mother found herself a job it was decided that he should go and live in Penang, with his uncle Ossie and aunt Addie and cousins Lesley and Priscilla. Although it was a wrench to be split up from his mother, it marked the beginning of perhaps the happiest part of his childhood and along with Lesley and Priscilla he revelled in the exotic surroundings and their Huckleberry Finn-like existence:

> We played in the neighbouring rubber plantations and hunted snakes. We came across all kinds of creatures including scorpions, giant centipedes and even plants

which could bite. The flying snakes scared me more than anything, including cobras. They had foldaway wings and would suddenly glide down from the trees. I remember we were playing a game one day when one of these snakes landed at my feet and I've never run so fast in my life.

Ashley was back at school again although he continued to make little progress, spending most of his time running wild with his friends. With his father dead and his mother away in Singapore, it was his left to his grandfather Scott to keep a watchful eye on him. But by the time he was eight, he was proving a handful for his guardians. Eventually, after ruining a nativity scene his grandfather had painstakingly built, it was decided he needed to be back with his mother, so he was packed off to Singapore. Although she had missed him, her son's arrival couldn't have come at a worse time, as both their lives were about to dramatically change.

After the war ended a number of enterprising British servicemen who had served out in the Far East decided to stay. They reasoned there were more opportunities for them than they would find back in Britain. One such man was a Yorkshireman called Hedley Haigh. He had been a sergeant with the Royal Artillery and opted to demobilize in Singapore after the war. He became manager of a cold storage company and it was while working there that he met Dulcie Jackson and the pair fell in love. When Ashley was reunited with his mother he was unaware of the new man in her life, but there was a more pressing matter in the form of school. Up to this point his education had been little short of shambolic so she decided he should go to a boarding school. It was run by Franciscan monks and was the same school Ashley's father and brothers had been to. If anyone could

West Nab and Deer Hill from Wessenden Head Moor.

bring his education up to scratch, they could. However it proved an unhappy experience all round. The monks were dismayed that he could barely read or write and Ashley hated it:

I was put in a dormitory with a group of upper-class Chinese boys and we were made to get up at five in the morning and take a cold shower before being made to kneel for an hour to chant prayers in the chapel.

He lasted just three weeks, at which point the monks decided to send him back to his mother, who found another day school in the hope that this might do the trick.

Although a widow, Dulcie was still a vivacious twenty-something and she had a string of admirers, including Haigh who Ashley still hadn't met. It took an accident that nearly left him an orphan, to finally bring them face-to-face. Haigh had been driving Dulcie through Singapore when an army lorry without lights smashed into them. She was badly injured and rushed to hospital. The family arrived from Penang and Ashley was taken to see his mother. When he got there "a dapper man with a strange accent and a trim little moustache" was already at her bedside. His mother recovered and after a few weeks she

The military funeral for Ashley's grandfather Scott.

Ashley's mother and stepfather, June 1950, Penang.

was back on her feet, although when Haigh was transferred to an office in Kuala Lumpur it appeared their relationship was over. However, she was undeterred and quit her job, joining him in the Malaysian capital with her bewildered son in tow. As she was no longer working their only income came from her pension, which meant living in a more humble house, with coconut leaves for a roof. Perhaps not surprisingly, Ashley fell further behind in class. He was sent to a local village school on the outskirts of the city, where he was the only European in a class full of Chinese and Malay children. Although he struggled in lessons the one thing he was good at was drawing and it was here that he first picked up a Chinese brush pen, which years later he used in his watercolours:

> All the local shopkeepers used them to do their accounts. They held the brush between two fingers and I used to watch them because I was fascinated by their speed and dexterity.

After just a year Ashley found himself being uprooted yet again. His mother and Haigh had become engaged and decided to move back to Penang. However, it wasn't a particularly happy homecoming. Although he was reunited with his cousins and grandfather, there was tension in the air. Haigh's job contract was not being renewed and he announced his intention to move to Yorkshire, where he planned to marry Dulcie. The Jacksons and Scotts, though, were Catholic families and insisted that if she was leaving Penang with him it was as a married woman. Haigh protested, arguing that his family back in England couldn't afford to travel all the way to Penang for a wedding, but in the face of their unyielding opposition he

The Railway Viaduct and River Dee near Stonehouse, Dentdale.

relented. In the weeks leading up to the big day, Haigh, a stern disciplinarian, spent time getting to know his future stepson. He was appalled that Ashley couldn't swim or play cricket (a must if he was to survive his childhood in Yorkshire) and set about giving him a crash-course in the finer arts of football, spin bowling and the front crawl. The wedding itself was held at a registry office followed by a reception at the Sea View Hotel, overlooking the beach at Penang. Ashley's grandfather Scott had organized a band to play, which ensured that proceedings went off with a bang.

It wasn't long before there were more tearful farewells as Ashley and his newly wed mother clambered aboard the *SS Canton*, bound for a new life in England. For Ashley, who was just nine years old, it meant yet more upheaval and uncertainty and he had no idea when he would next see his grandfather and his cousins. Malaya was the only place that had really felt like home and with his memories of Scotland still fresh in his mind it was with particular sadness that he waved goodbye.

Clive and Sonny Boy stood shouting and waving on the quayside while his grandfather Scott played his accordion as the ship manoeuvred away from its berth. As his grandfather slowly slipped from view Ashley could just make out the fading strains of *We'll Meet Again*, but this proved to be the last time they would see one another.

The route across the Indian Ocean, through the Red Sea and up the Suez Canal had become a familiar one to Ashley who had already seen more of the world than many people do in a lifetime. While on board his stepfather taught him how to play table tennis and said that Ashley should from now on use his middle name 'Norman' as he considered Ashley too effeminate for a child soon to be growing up in Yorkshire. This did not bother the youngster as it meant taking his father's name. Finally, after six weeks at sea, the verdant slopes of the English coastline emerged through the early summer morning mist as they approached Southampton. It was June 1950, and here he was once again, in a new country, with a new name.

# 4

# Welcome to Yorkshire

Haigh's parents lived in the village of Linthwaite, a few miles outside Huddersfield overlooking the Colne Valley. But rather than head straight north they travelled by train to London as they were awaiting another important arrival – Haigh's much cherished car, a black bull-nose Morris Eight which he had shipped across from Malaya. Ashley's first visit to the capital brought a mixed reaction:

We went to see the original production of the musical *Oklahoma!* and I was bought a cowboy outfit and marched round the West End wearing a large Stetson.

But despite the bright lights and the glamour the fumes from the buses reminded him of Glasgow and he yearned to be back in Penang.

The Morris finally arrived and Ashley, his mother and his new stepfather began the journey north. They finally pulled up outside a next-to-end terrace on Hazel Grove where Ashley's stepfather was reunited with his parents and younger brother, Malcolm, who he had not seen since before the war. His parents then turned to inspect the new bride and stepson he had brought with him from the Far East. Despite the awkwardness of the situation and the fact their new daughter-in-law had been married before and came with a son, they welcomed Ashley and his mother into their family. They lived with the Haighs' for the next few months and Ashley started a friendship with Malcolm, who was a year older, that still lasts today. Ashley vividly remembers the night he first set foot on Yorkshire soil:

I could not believe my eyes that night, it was dark when we arrived and I went to the back of the house and looked across at the valley which was all lit up, it looked like a kind of fairyland.

But if Ashley's home life appeared stable, school continued to be a miserable experience. He enrolled at a local junior school in the village, where his lack of reading and writing skills made him an easy target:

I was placed in a class taught by a man who believed very strongly in corporal punishment and he made my life a misery. He spoke with a very broad accent and I couldn't

Watercolour Memories of Yorkshire, Wolfstones Holme Valley.

understand a word he said, it was like Chinese to me. So he used to drag me out of the class and give me a good hiding. But I didn't say anything, I was too scared to tell my mother.

The beatings continued until two sisters in his class, upset by what was happening, told their mother who spoke to Ashley's mum. She then marched to the school to complain about her son's treatment. Despite her intervention the beatings continued, albeit less frequently.

For a young lad who had lived most of his life in the Far East, Yorkshire came as something of a culture shock:

The thing that amazed me more than anything else was seeing a white man lifting a dustbin and driving a bus, because in Malaysia you never saw any white people, whatever background they came from, doing menial jobs. If you were white you got the best jobs and you went straight to the top of the queue.

He remembers talking to his step-grandmother who wanted to know how long it took him to learn to wear shoes and speak English:

She was asking all these questions, but we had flushing toilets back in Malaya when they still had outside toilets over here. There was no hot water, or bathrooms in most people's houses and you think, well who's the more civilized? My mother used to take photographs of our back yard to send to Penang and Singapore and my Uncle Tommy wrote back one time and said, 'Is this what the bombs did?'

As the months wore on Ashley gradually found his feet. He was accepted by the local kids and it was here that he began his life-long fascination with the Pennine hills of Yorkshire:

At night I would gaze out of my bedroom window at the starlit hills because it was all new to me. In Malaya you didn't get distant horizons because the land was flat and blocked by lines of trees and bushes.

When winter came and the fields were frozen he would go sledging with Malcolm and in the summer he went on trips with the Boy Scouts and played cricket and rugby. But while Ashley was able to adapt to life in West Yorkshire, his mother struggled:

We had a colonial background and then suddenly we arrived in this new world. My mother had never washed a dish in her life and she'd never cooked. She was used to going to parties but that was it.

Then Haigh, who was working in the office of an abattoir in Huddersfield, announced they were moving to their own house in nearby Milnsbridge. Their new home consisted of two upstairs rooms and one downstairs. To go to the outside toilet, which they shared with five other people, they had to walk twenty yards down a narrow ginnel. It was a far cry from the conditions they enjoyed in Malaya and Ashley's mother, who was now pregnant with her second child, struggled to cope with being an ordinary, working-class Yorkshire housewife.

Following the move, Ashley had also switched schools which put an end to the misery of Linthwaite. But while he had escaped the clutches of his former schoolmaster, he found his stepfather an equally strict disciplinarian who didn't shirk from giving him a good hiding if he saw fit. Nevertheless, he felt increasingly at home playing in the surrounding hills:

A group of us used to walk up to Crosland Moor and play cricket. I would look out across the Colne Valley and watch the trains going by like little miniature Hornby dublos heading down the valley towards Manchester. It probably sounds corny, but even back then I felt like there was a spirit calling me in.

He joined in games with the other kids. One of their favourite pastimes was swimming in their own free, outdoor heated pool:

We used to go to a local canal that ran near Factory Lane where Joe Hyman's mills pumped out hot water which was used to wash the fibres that made up the fabrics. It may have been a bit tainted but it didn't do us any harm.

A gang of them used to break into the mills when they were closed by balancing on the pipes laid across the canal and climbing through the spikes put up to deter intruders:

It's funny, because years later I was commissioned to paint the very same mills. Mr Hyman wanted the painting as a birthday gift for his wife and one of the bosses at the firm took me onto the hills to point out the best perspective

and tell me about the area. I think he was a bit shocked when I told him how well I knew the place already. It was great to be asked to come back and paint these mills where I used to play as a kid. But the sad thing now is that a lot of those chimneys have been pulled down and we've lost that wonderful Lowry landscape, because those chimneys were a kind of homage to the people who worked in them.

Ashley's school life was also starting to shows signs of improvement. He found New Street School much more to his liking and joined the local Baptist Church Boy Scout troop, which he took a shine to, becoming leader of Cuckoo Patrol. He continued to struggle academically, but his one saving grace was art and he found himself increasingly drawn towards the petrified swells of the Pennine hills:

I wanted to paint them effectively and Hedley, in one of his generous moments, bought me a paintbox. But the effort to turn the daubs into real paintings was slow and I found it almost as difficult as learning to read, but I enjoyed it and it was the one thing I thought I could be good at.

Just as he was starting to feel settled there was more upheaval. Ashley's mother gave birth to her second child, Geoffrey, and then his stepfather was handed a new job as manager of Barnsley Abattoir, which meant moving yet again. This time they landed in Longman Road, Barnsley, in a spacious Victorian semi-detached that reflected their newfound social status. The only drawback was that it had just two bedrooms, his mother

The Approaching Storm, Swaledale Moor.

Evening Light, Langsett Moor to Cut Gate.

and stepfather shared one and Geoffrey had the other, leaving Ashley to make do with the attic. Although it was cold during winter it at least gave him the opportunity to carry on painting in peace.

Another bit of good fortune brought about by changing schools was that he was spared the agony of having to sit his eleven-plus exam, not that life at his new school was a piece of cake. Holyrood Roman Catholic School had a reputation as being the toughest in town and years later while teaching inmates at Wakefield Prison, Ashley discovered that several of those serving sentences were old Holyrood boys. His first day at school was something of a rite of passage. It was arranged that a lad called Hugh, who lived nearby, would walk with him to school and show him the ropes. But at break time, as Ashley was trying to get used to yet another school yard, Hugh told him casually that he would be fighting Paddy, the unofficial 'cock of the school', at lunchtime:

Here I was the new boy who spoke with this BBC accent and the next thing I know is I'm told I have to fight the hardest kid at the school. I'd played rough and tumble in Malaya with the Chinese and Indian kids, but we never fought one another.

At the allotted time a small crowd of schoolchildren gathered behind the back yard jostling each other for the best vantage point to see the scrap:

If I ran off then I would have been a target for every bully in the school so there was no getting out of it. I think I threw the first punch in the end because I thought, 'What

the heck'. But he was bigger than me and he ended up kneeling on top of me and he was about to give me another crack when he looked at me and said, 'What are we fighting for, I don't even bloody know thee?'

The fight ended with both boys' playground reputations intact, although for eleven-year-old Ashley it was a more painful start to his new life in Barnsley than he had been hoping for. Following his combative welcome he decided school was about survival, rather than enjoyment:

It was a rough school, not because of bad behaviour, but the children who went there tended to come from the poorer parts of town, their fathers worked down the pits. There was no way I could have a name like Ashley so I stuck with 'Norman' and I made sure the other kids didn't find out that I liked to paint.

Despite his fractured education he had been placed in the top class:

Lord knows why. I was always good at talking but academically I was bloody hopeless, because I had never stayed in one school long enough.

Perhaps not surprisingly he struggled to begin with. But if art was a saving grace then so, too, was Gertrude Young. Most of us remember at least one teacher with particular affection and for Ashley this was his form mistress at Holyrood. She started giving him after-school tuition and slowly he began to flourish:

She must have spotted something in me that she felt was worth persevering with and I owe her a big debt of gratitude, because she was the first teacher who had ever given me any self-confidence and told me that I was any good.

He prospered outside the classroom, too:

All the hours of practice my stepfather had forced me into meant I was reasonably good at sport, particularly swimming. I made a few of the school squads and because of Holyrood's fearsome reputation we usually beat the other teams we played, something we relished – particularly when we beat Barnsley Grammar School.

By the time he was fifteen Ashley had been elevated to head boy and found himself increasingly absorbed in painting. He started taking extra art lessons after school and one of his posters won a road safety competition. Weekends, too, were taken up by sketching:

On Saturday mornings I used to go with a couple of lads, who also liked to draw, and walk up to a place called Wentworth, which is a training college now, and paint the gatehouse.

Other times he would get the train to Edale and walk back over to Langsett, with his sketchbook in hand.

But while his school life was finally improving, the situation at home remained fraught as he continued to clash with his stepfather.

I loved Holyrood, that was my little world because my home life wasn't a particularly happy one. I used to walk in and I'd sit there and say nothing for fear of saying the wrong thing and getting whacked.

I'd have an argument with my mother and he would come in and give me the biggest bloody hiding of my life. And then she would be screaming, 'Don't hit him, don't hit him.' I took a few good whacks but you get used to it after a while, although in the end I became quite introverted.

Looking back at his stepfather's behaviour he believes it was an attempt, albeit a cruel one at times, to toughen him up:

I went back to the place where we used to live not long ago and it felt like a haunted house because it still had all those bad memories for me. I won't ever forget what I went through.

It was years later before Ashley won his stepfather's approval:

The greatest accolade he ever gave me was when he came to our house in Holmfirth which we'd just bought. He looked around and said, 'You've done alright lad.' And I thought, 'Bloody hell, I've cracked him.'

Haigh imposed a strict curfew on Ashley, meaning he had to be back home before nine o'clock, which, once he'd finished his art classes, didn't leave much time for meeting his friends, or girls. Like many other teenagers growing up in Britain during the 1950s, he had to wait for the weekly pilgrimage to the local cinema for the chance to meet members of the opposite sex:

A bunch of us would go and watch the matinee. I yearned to be like Tony Daley – he smoked, dressed like Frank Sinatra and he wore a trench coat and all the girls flocked round him. I fancied a ginger-haired girl called Janet McPherson and one day I plucked up the courage to ask if she'd like to sit next to me in the cinema, but she wasn't interested.

Although his home life was strained at times it wasn't always an unhappy one. His mother loved music and the whispering strains of Lionel Hampton, Ella Fitzgerald and Frank Sinatra could often be heard drifting down Longman Road. The true happiness of his mother, who gave birth to two more children, was wrapped around a wistful nostalgia for her former life:

She was a lovely person but it was difficult for her coming to live in England. She used to talk to me about 'the good old days', and I think even up to the very day she died she dreamt she would someday go back to the Far East.

He admits there was always a distance between the two of them:

I never really got close to my mum and she never got close to me. I suppose it started when I was a kid because when she was in Singapore I was in Penang. But a few days before she died I went to her see and told her I loved her and I'm glad I did, because wouldn't that be terrible to never have told your mum you love her?

Ashley left school at the age of fifteen with his heart set on winning a place at Barnsley Art School. But that meant passing an exam, which despite his academic improvement, was by no means a certainty. It was Oswald Livesey, Holyrood's headmaster, and Miss Netherwood, his art teacher, who came to his rescue. They gave glowing references to the art school's principal, Harry Glover, who, having examined Ashley's portfolio, offered him a place without him needing to sit the dreaded exam:

If I hadn't been accepted I really don't know what I would have done, because I didn't have a plan B.

Down from Wessenden.

He threw himself into as many different courses as he could find – from commercial painting and decorating, to fine art:

I practically lived there day and night during the week, I just felt completely at home there.

However, he needed to start earning some money and contributing to the household bills, which meant finding some work. He heard that a man called Derek Harley was looking for an apprentice signwriter so he asked him for a job and to his surprise he took him on. It meant Ashley was now working full-time and spending five evenings a week studying at art school. The night before he started his new job his stepfather pulled him to one side and warned him to watch out for any 'funny business' from the other workmen. He didn't quite know what he was getting at and turned up promptly for work the next day impeccably dressed in bright, white overalls, an apron and gleaming black boots. The building site was a swarm of bricklayers, plumbers and carpenters who, when they found out it was Ashley's first day, put him through the initiation ceremony that awaited all new starters.

They pinned me to the ground and ripped off my trousers and painted my penis with pink emulsion and coated my testicles in thick varnish. I washed the emulsion off but I had to shave my pubic hairs to get rid of the varnish. I threw my underpants away and I didn't breathe a word of what happened at home.

Although he was supposed to be an apprentice he didn't lay his hands on a brush for a long time. Instead, he was given all the lousy jobs that nobody else wanted, like scraping the muck off guttering and drainpipes so they were ready for painting. It was hard, unsatisfying work and he returned home filthy and exhausted, all for a weekly wage of just two pounds. But this meagre salary lasted less than a year as the firm he was working for ran out of jobs and he was laid off. He returned to art school and became a full-time student again. But having tasted what it was like to earn his own money, he wanted more of it. He just had to find someone else willing to take on a young apprentice.

# 5

# The Apprentice Signwriter

There weren't many specialist signwriters in Yorkshire in 1957 and there were fewer still in Barnsley. But in his hunt for work there was one name that kept cropping up; Ron Darwent:

Other painters and signwriters talked about him with grudging admiration. He was the best for miles around, a real artist and master of his craft.

Ashley turned up at his studio at the top of Sheffield Road to see if he would take him on as his apprentice. Initially Darwent declined, saying he was happier working on his own. But Ashley persisted and eventually he gave in.

'He pestered me for a job but I was the same when I started out and he reminded me a bit of myself,' Darwent recalls.

'I wasn't looking to take anyone on but I took to the lad straight away and he proved to be good. He was very keen, hard working and reliable and we've been pals ever since.'

Darwent's own boss, Jim Croft, had been the first specialist signwriter in Barnsley. Most of the work back then was done by skilled painters and decorators who didn't have any qualifications, as Darwent remembers:

With signwriting and gilding you find there's always somebody watching you and I remember this chap saying to my boss, 'I love watching you work, you're very good. I suppose you're very well qualified?' and my boss said, 'Yes I am.' And the chap asked, 'Well what's your top qualification?' He said, 'I've got the best one,' 'What's that?', 'I can do' job.'

At the age of sixteen Ashley became Darwent's apprentice, earning the princely sum of one shilling and one penny an hour. To begin with he was only given basic tasks:

When Ashley started he couldn't do a right lot, so I'd have him doing a second coat of lettering or a bit of shading.

Not that this bothered his young apprentice:

I loved it. Every morning I had to arrive at his studio an hour before him and clean the place out. But he also set up a practice area for me and for part of that hour I could use his gear to try and learn, choosing one letter and doing it over and over again until it was good enough to get a nod of approval from the boss when he came in.

These days signwriting has virtually become a redundant trade, replaced by ready-made computerized logos. But back then it was a necessary and much sought after craft and between them Ashley and Darwent did around ninety per cent of all the commercial signwriting in Barnsley. They were responsible for the gilding of all the big high street shops in the town, including Littlewoods, Marks & Spencer and Woolworths. And when the weather was bad they began working for the local transport and haulage firms, lettering coaches and buses, as Ashley recalls:

When we were out on a job we used to always try and work on what we called the sunny side in the morning, because if you were working outside it could get cold, especially if you were forty foot up a church on scaffolding doing some lettering. It was hard work but it was enjoyable and it taught me how to work outside.

When you put paint on to vertical glass inside so that it reads correctly from the outside, the paint jumps off the brush because of the static on the windows. So you have to do this very quickly, but at the same you've got to be in control of the brush otherwise you'll end up with a right mess.

It was good training for his watercolours:

When you're using water on glass you slide everywhere, but in painting as soon as your brush hits the paper there's

Ashley at work as a signwriter.

suction which makes it easier and because of my signwriting skills I was able to work with confidence on paper.

The pair enjoyed working together, although Darwent admits there were a few occasions when jobs went wrong:

I think I was on holiday at the time so I'd sent him to do a job for Woolworths. Ashley had the task of designing a couple of posters each saying, 'Spot the deliberate mistake in the window! Valuable prizes given away free.' He got cracking and the posters were put up in the window. But the next day the manager was angry because Ashley had spelt 'valuable' wrong and he went up to him and said, 'You're making us look a laughing stock, we've had half the town coming in and claiming this prize.'

Spelling was never Ashley's strong point – a legacy from his school days – but he wasn't the only one to slip up, as Darwent recalls:

There was another occasion when he'd been doing the lettering on a van for a building firm and the owner's son, who was the managing director, complained that he'd got the name wrong on the side of the van. I always told Ashley to write down what the customer wanted and to keep it, because then you've got proof. Ashley insisted he'd written what the son told him and it turned out it was the owner's son who'd made the mistake. I remember Ashley saying, 'Well, if the managing director doesn't know what his firm's called how does he expect me to

know?' And after that the owner was quite apologetic.

But Darwent admits there were other occasions when they simply had to hold their hands up and admit they had made a mistake:

You always got comments from people when you were signwriting, somebody would shout, 'You're spelling it wrong' and you just ignored it because normally they were winding you up. But one time we were writing the words 'British Legion' on a big gable end and me and Ashley were on a plank about thirty foot up and somebody shouted, 'You're spelling it wrong,' but we didn't pay any attention. It was only when we got down that we noticed we'd missed the 't' out of British, so we had to start all over again.

Over the next few years the pair became good friends, with Darwent becoming a father-like figure to Ashley, replacing the one he never knew:

Ron would talk to me as an equal, he listened patiently to my problems and my ambitions and he always offered sound advice.

It was also Darwent who opened Ashley's eyes to large swathes of the Yorkshire landscape he had never seen before:

He loved to go hiking or rock climbing at weekends and he started to invite me along. I'd been around the hills near where I lived but I'd not ventured out into the wilds

The Lyke Wake Walk with Ron Darwent (top, second left),
Ashley front centre.

and it was a revelation to me. Ron took me to the really remote and spectacular parts of the Dales and I was just mesmerized by the sheer size and sullen beauty of the landscape.

Ashley's friendship with Darwent was a godsend at a time when his relationship with his stepfather was going from bad to worse. Haigh allowed him to go to night school but weekend trips to the cinema and the youth club were forbidden, which meant that Darwent's studio became a haven for him. The work continued to flood in and there was plenty of overtime because lorries and vans could only be lettered outside normal working hours:

Some weeks I clocked up sixty-four hours and I would take home more than three pounds and ten shillings, in old money.

Not that he could spend it. Every penny was handed over to his stepfather, who put it towards the household bills. It wasn't until he was nearly eighteen that he was finally allowed a small, weekly allowance.

It was while he was working for Darwent that a figure from Ashley's past re-appeared suddenly. His mother's younger brother Clive, who he'd played truant with in his days back in Scotland, turned up at the house one day. He had spent several years in the Merchant Navy and arrived in Barnsley in the hope of finding a new job:

He had visited all kinds of exotic places and I listened carefully to the tales of his exploits in the bars of South America and the Far East.

Ashley was allowed to show him round Barnsley and in return he hoped Clive would reveal the knack of how to impress girls, which had hitherto eluded him:

He taught me how to chat a girl up even though I didn't always understand his patter.

The other thing Clive gave him, which he had also been lacking, was a bit of style:

I wasn't even allowed to wear long trousers until I left school so I'd never had any cool clothes before. But I got all his cast-offs. He gave me this wonderful, white sharkskin bomber jacket and a silk jockey jacket with 'Singapore' written across the back and suddenly I looked like one of the trendiest kids in Barnsley.

But Clive didn't hang around for long. Ashley's mother had helped get him a job at the local pit, but on his first day he lasted just six hours:

He came up from the pit and shook his head saying, 'That place is like a concentration camp. I've never worked so hard in my life.'

Having decided that life in Barnsley wasn't for him he headed straight back to the Merchant Navy.

Although Ashley was sad to see him go, his uncle had given him the confidence to spread his wings a little. As well as spending his days signwriting and his nights studying at art classes, he was finally allowed to go to the local youth club where he was able to show off his jive skills. His mother had taught him how to dance while his stepfather was out and he found he had a passion for the bop. He teamed up with a girl called Dolores Nightingale and together they won several competitions, travelling at weekends with their friends from Holyrood to places as far away as Blackpool to compete against other youth groups. He even joined a Lonnie Donegan-style skiffle group, like countless other teenagers up and down the land. Girls, though, remained a mystery to him and apart from a fleeting kiss from a girl in a hay barn one summer holiday in

A young Ashley in Blackpool 1958.

Ireland his teenage fantasies remained nothing more than that. But his life was about to change – and it was all to do with a nude woman.

A model was brought in for pupils to draw in the fine art class one evening at college. Ashley sat on the floor to draw a close up of the naked woman, who was sitting in a Windsor chair. When the tutor came back in he marched him off to the principal's office together with his unfinished work.

As punishment he was made to paint the art school gates. This humiliation was made bearable by the fact that all the girls from the neighbouring Barnsley Technical School had to pass through them on their way to class. One girl, in particular, caught his eye. She was fifteen, petite, blue-eyed and to the smitten teenager watching her she seemed to glide rather than walk. He made the job last longer than it should have done just so he could catch another burning glimpse. He didn't muster the courage to talk to her but he found out her name, Anne Hutchinson.

During the ensuing days and weeks he tried to think of ways of engineering a meeting but to no avail. As luck would have it, though, she turned up at a reunion dance run by Holyrood School for its former pupils. He spotted her across the room and went over to ask if she would like to dance. She agreed and after the party was over he walked her back home. The following week, messages were passed between the two of them via friends as neither of their families had telephones. Anne's parents agreed to let her go on a date, providing her eleven-year-old sister, Una, went along, too.

The three of us took the bus to Stocksbridge and they watched while I did some sketches. To this day I still have the painting that came out of those sketches.

But after just a few dates Anne was struck down with a virus and spent several weeks in and out of hospital, putting their fledgling courtship in jeopardy. Ashley had not yet met her parents and wasn't sure he would be welcome turning up on her doorstep unannounced, even if it was to see how she was. A friend of his, Jim Moran, listened to his dilemma and volunteered to go with him to Anne's house on a council estate in Dodworth.

Her dad opened the door. Most parents would have probably told me to clear off but he invited us both inside. It turned out that their television set was faulty and Jim happened to be training as a television engineer and he fixed it, which put us in their good books.

Anne soon recovered and they continued seeing each other, usually with Una acting as chaperone. In those days relationships moved at a more sedate pace which probably pleased the parents, but did nothing for teenage desires. Then one summer Ashley was invited on a family holiday to Great Yarmouth, a sign that Anne's parents, Donald and Elsie, had accepted their courtship. Although the sleeping arrangements weren't quite what Ashley had in mind:

I ended up sleeping in a room with her father the whole time we were there. So I shared a bed with him long before I ever slept with Anne.

By now, the young couple were deeply in love and spent much of the holiday holding hands and enjoying long walks on the beach, albeit under her parents' watchful gaze. During the trip Ashley painted a couple of pictures of the Broads, and when they returned home he took them to Holyrood Youth Club, which was run by a priest called Father McNamara who bought one for ten shillings. It was the first painting he had ever sold.

While his relationship with Anne blossomed, Ashley's home life remained volatile:

Sometimes my stepfather was kind, he would take me along with his pals to concerts featuring big names like Count Basie and Lionel Hampton at the City Hall in Sheffield. But on the other hand, one wrong word could result in a beating. Anne was a regular visitor to our

A painting Ashley made for Anne on their first date.

house by this time and she was appalled by the way he treated me.

The situation came to a head one New Year's Day. Ashley and Anne had been out the night before. So, too, had his mother and stepfather, leaving a fourteen-year-old girl to babysit Ashley's young half-sister. The next day he returned from visiting Anne to find his mother in an agitated state, saying that his stepfather had accused him of 'getting up to monkey business' with the babysitter:

It was ridiculous and totally unfounded. I was twenty years old, I was madly in love with Anne and the babysitter was just a kid. My mother had just finished talking as Hedley walked into the kitchen and all the pent up anger and unhappiness just exploded in my head. I hurled myself at him and gave him the kind of good hiding he had dished out to me so often and I told him exactly what I thought of him.

Although their subsequent relationship remained strained it was the last time his stepfather raised a fist against him. And for Ashley, it put an end to years of torment.

His relationship with Anne continued to flourish and after a five-year courtship they announced their engagement. They had saved up enough money to get married but a family row threatened to ruin their wedding plans. Ashley's mother insisted it should be a Roman Catholic ceremony, otherwise she wouldn't attend. While Anne's father, an Anglican, was proving equally stubborn, claiming he would never walk his daughter down the aisle of a Catholic church. Both families

Featherbed Moss, Langsett Moor.

A young Ashley and Anne on the seafront at Yarnmouth in 1958.

He talked to her about their wedding dilemma at which point she asked to speak to Ashley alone. It's a conversation he has never forgotten:

She knew it would almost certainly be the last time we would see each other and she told me to get married in whatever church we wanted. She also told me that I had to keep on painting, 'Show 'em, Norman, show 'em.' Those words have echoed down the years and I've lost count of the times they've helped pick me up.

Ashley returned to Barnsley determined to face up to both families and resolve the marriage dispute, but as it happened the problem sorted itself out – with a little divine

Ashley with Anne in the early 60s.

rejected the idea of a registry office leaving the young couple wondering what on earth they should do. But amid all the arguments Ashley received an urgent message from Limerick, telling him that his grandmother was seriously ill. He and Anne used the money they had been saving up to fly to Ireland where they visited her in hospital. The reunion was an emotional one for Ashley:

I was so proud to be able to introduce Anne but I was shocked to see how ill she looked.

The opening of the gallery in Barnsley, which is now the art shop on Church Street.

Ashley turned up in a Ford van driven by his boss Ron Darwent, who was best man, much to the dismay of the photographer:

I remember he just looked at us and said, 'I can't take a picture of you arriving in a bloody van,' so he told us to stand by the church door instead.

The reception was held at Anne's house and the catering was done by her mother. Despite a shortage of cash they cobbled together enough for a short honeymoon – a four-night break in Blackpool. It meant they could spend Christmas alone together without the usual family hassles. It marked, too, the beginning of a new chapter in their lives where suddenly now, anything seemed possible.

intervention. Anne's father had been pondering the situation on his way home one day when he spotted a Catholic priest visiting a nearby house. Impulsively he walked over to him and asked if he would call in and have a chat with him. The priest happily obliged and afterwards Ashley's father-in-law-to-be relented and agreed to a Catholic wedding.

The couple were married at Holyrood Catholic Church on December 22, 1962. But following the expensive trip to Ireland Ashley had little money left and rather than paying for taxis to take guests to and from the church he asked those friends that had cars to help out. So instead of arriving in style

Sketch of Ashley's gallery in Barnsley.

# 6

# Portrait of a Struggling Artist

The newlyweds returned from their honeymoon and took up residence at 27 New Street, in Dodworth. Ashley continued working with Darwent, but following the success of his first exhibition in Brighouse he was now more determined than ever to become a professional artist. Over the next eighteen months he spent all his spare time practising his watercolour technique as the commissions started trickling in. Most of the time he was asked to create romantic 'chocolate box' impressions of someone's holiday cottage in the Dales, which while hardly being an artistic challenge was all grist to the mill. The snippets of publicity he had garnered helped generate more interest, but if he was going to be a professional artist he couldn't simply rely on social clubs and the occasional exhibition to showcase his paintings to the public. He needed his own premises.

It was Anne's father who came up with the answer. He knew the landlord of the Thornley Arms pub in Dodworth, which happened to be next to a disused barn that was available to rent for £1 a week:

It was a big outbuilding with two floors, including an

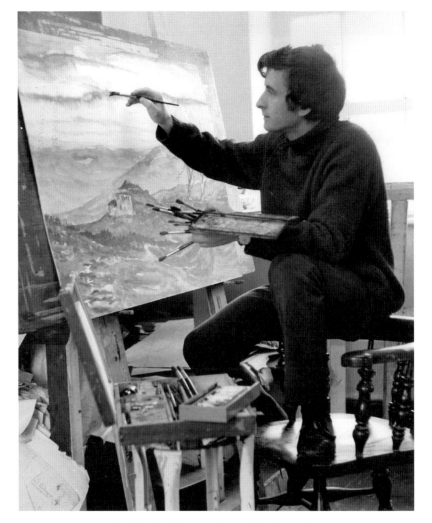

Ashley in his studio at Dodworth.

Greenfield Moor.

upstairs area where I could do my work. There was an old coke stove and when I lit the thing it would smoke the whole place out. It needed a hell of a lot of work but it was just what I needed.

This was the biggest decision of my life. I talked to Anne about it and we worked out that we could just about afford it as long as I was still able to do signwriting jobs.

As 1964 drew to a close he took the plunge, which meant he would have to quit his job. But Darwent wasn't only his boss, having worked together for nearly eight years he had become one of his closest friends:

It took me a long time to summon up the courage to tell him. I remember we were lettering some Barnsley Brewery vehicles and I suddenly blurted out that I had to leave.

He had talked to Darwent before about his dream of becoming a watercolour artist and his employer had always been supportive:

He didn't bat an eyelid, even when I said I would have to do some signwriting to survive, although I promised I wouldn't take any work off him. We always said we wouldn't take work off each other and we never did.

Darwent is proud of what his former apprentice has gone on to achieve:

He was good at the job there's no doubt about it, but he wanted to be an artist. When people say he's done well for himself, I say, 'Aye, he has, but he's worked hard to do it.' He painted in the evenings after he finished work and that's what I've always admired about him, he's always been prepared to work hard.

He says Ashley showed smart business sense from the very beginning:

He was quite clever when I look back, because after we finished a job he would give one of his paintings to the boss who would put it in his office. It was good business, but most people today wouldn't dream of giving stuff away like that, they want the money straight away. But he didn't, he worked his way in and it paid dividends for him later.

Darwent admits that he initially had doubts about whether Ashley would be able to earn a living from his watercolours:

When he got started I thought he had guts because I couldn't see anyone making a living out of being an artist in Barnsley in those days. It wasn't as if he started as an artist with a good few years training behind him. He didn't have much experience, but he proved me wrong. If you look at his paintings today they capture the mood of the landscape, particularly his moorland scenes, and few artists are really able to do that.

For Ashley, leaving his friend to set up on his own had been a tough decision and now he had to work twice as hard. Firstly he had to keep the signwriting jobs coming in and secondly he had to get his studio up and running and somehow establish himself as an artist:

It was a daunting prospect because when I left Ron nobody knew anything about Ashley Jackson or his paintings.

To begin with he concentrated on bringing some money in by doing any work that came his way, which usually meant prosaic jobs like lettering cattle trucks and oil tankers. However, on one occasion he became the talk of the town.

I got a call from the Barnsley Corporation asking me to give them a quote for gilding the letters on the cenotaph at the town hall. I just thought it was pals of mine who were playing a joke, so I didn't ring back.

But I got another couple of messages and eventually I rang up and this voice said, 'Aren't you bothered about the job then?' And I said, 'Bloody hell, I thought you were one of my friends playing a prank.'

I agreed to do the job and they asked what I needed and I told them a long ladder and a couple of sandbags to put at the bottom.

These duly arrived and Ashley sized in the letters:

It was a lovely hot day and I thought, 'I can't gild it yet,' so I carried the ladder and hid it down an alley next to the town hall out of sight because there was no way I was

carting it all the way back home.

As he was returning early the next morning he decided it was a good idea to move the sandbags:

I climbed up the cenotaph and wedged them in the floodlights near the top so that vandals couldn't nick them and I went home.

He had barely stepped through his front door when the phone rang:

It was a police inspector from Barnsley and he said, 'Ashley, have you been working in Barnsley today?' and I said, 'Yes I've working in front of the town hall,' and I told him where I'd put these sandbags and he listened and said, 'Somebody's reported seeing a bomb and we've got Barnsley centre sealed off, can you come and move them?' I said I would but I waited until it was getting dark because I didn't want to turn up and everyone to say, 'That's the daft sod who stopped all the traffic.'

It had taken a lot of sweat and hard work but as 1966 dawned Ashley was finally able to open his studio, a year since his debut in Brighouse. Having quickly realized the importance of publicity, he rang round the local newspapers to see if they might be interested in writing a story about an impecunious young artist who had opened a studio and gallery in a Yorkshire mining village. Several reporters rolled up along with a few locals, curious to see what all the fuss was about, and sure enough a few articles appeared in the press.

Storm over Garsdale.

Coping with the pressure of signwriting and looking after his studio meant he was regularly working sixteen-hour days. But his hard work was rewarded when the curator of Newark Art Gallery offered him a one-man exhibition, not just for a single day but for two weeks. He drove down to Nottinghamshire armed with thirty paintings, including seven he'd already sold that he had to borrow back.

All the paintings were impressions of the Yorkshire Dales which I'd worked from sketching sessions along the rainswept Buttertubs Pass that John Wesley had once ridden across. The rest were scenes of Swaledale, the misty heights of Wensleydale and Arkengarthdale.

The prices ranged from three guineas to fifteen for a study of the Tan Hill pub. Much to his delight, he sold the lot.

Finally, it seemed his supporters were beginning to outnumber his detractors. One of his earliest admirers was local artist Stanley Chapman, a tall spindly man with a perpetual smile on his face, who attended Ashley's first exhibition in Brighouse. It was Chapman who urged him to try and become a fellow of The Royal Society of Arts, which he did. This was another feather in his cap but if he was going to reach a wider audience he needed to get a foothold in London. His first attempt proved unsuccessful. He drove down to the Royal Academy and submitted three paintings to be considered for its annual exhibition. These were rejected, but undeterred he came up with another plan; one that he hoped would get the press interested:

I thought if the Royal Academy won't have me then I would stage my own exhibition on the pavement by Westminster Bridge.

He rang round his growing band of press contacts to let them know what he was doing and find out whether they might want to run a story:

A week later I was in my studio and this guy came in. He wandered round for a minute and then asked if he could use my phone, so I said, 'Yes'. I heard him saying, 'Yeah, I'm in his studio and he's well worth promoting.' The guy told me he was from the BBC and handed the phone over to me saying his boss would like to have a word. I picked up the receiver and explained that I was going down to London the following Saturday which happened to be July 30, the date of England's World Cup final match against West Germany. The guy on the phone said, 'I'm going to put Keith Macklin on the line because he'll come and meet you and do an interview.'

It was the stroke of luck he'd been hoping for. The following weekend he packed some paintings into the back of his van and set off for London along with two friends, Jack Brown and Peter Midwood:

By the time we got there it was nearly dusk and we managed to get parked up in a back yard somewhere in Chelsea. We heard that England had won the match and made our way down to Trafalgar Square.

Here they were greeted by scenes not seen in the capital since VE Day:

I'd never seen anything like it, there were people everywhere, they were even running across the top of cars but nobody was bothered. The noise was incredible, all you could hear were chants of 'England, England'.

It was unbelievable, there was a sea of people everywhere you looked, the atmosphere sent shivers down your spine, and I'm not even a football fan.

Ashley brought his harmonica with him and Midwood had his guitar so the three of them took advantage of the carnival atmosphere by busking round Chelsea's pubs:

We didn't have any money with us so we went into the boozers playing for free pints, which wasn't difficult because England had just won the World Cup.

After singing themselves hoarse and drinking themselves into a stupor they staggered back to the van, which was their bed for the night, somehow managing to avoid putting their feet through the canvases. The following morning they dragged themselves down to Westminster Bridge, where a throng of people were still celebrating from the night before:

We set up my paintings near the House of Commons down by the river when all of sudden a squad car drove over and a policeman got out and asked us if we had a permit. I apologized saying I'd left it at home, knowing fine well that I didn't really have one.

By now a large crowd had gathered but just as it looked as though the officer was going to make them move on, the TV crew arrived:

Keith said to the policeman, 'You don't think the BBC would come without a permit, do you?' This seemed to keep the officer happy and he even got a couple of his colleagues to rope off an area so I could be interviewed.

The following day the interview went out on the BBC's *Nationwide* programme. So although he returned home without having sold any paintings, his TV exposure had given him the vital oxygen of publicity.

Having made initial breakthrough, he made a point of ringing round the local and national newspapers whenever he had an exhibition lined up:

I was a cheeky so-and-so, I would ring up the *Daily Mirror* and the *Daily Express* and say, 'May I speak to the editor please?' and I'd get through to their secretaries and I'd say, 'My name's Ashley Jackson, I'm the Yorkshire artist,' and they would put me through. The editors all said the same thing, that they admired my nerve but there was no news in watercolours, I had to do something out of the ordinary. But to a man they all said, 'Next time you're doing something give me a call' and bingo, I'd made some important contacts.

Over the ensuing eighteen months his career moved steadily, if not spectacularly. He enjoyed a couple of exhibitions, including one at The Federation of British Artists, in London, featuring artists from the Royal Institute of Painters in Water Colours (RI):

> I remember walking in to one of the exhibition previews and they'd hung my work right on the line, which means right on your eye level in the best position.

His painting was flanked by a Sir William Russell Flint on one side and a Rowland Hilder on the other. Each artist was asked to put their name above their work and just for good measure Ashley had written his in big, bold letters so you could still see it even from the back of the room. He continued to get his name in the newspapers, but headlines don't pay the bills and his were mounting. He was trying to live up to his self-styled image as a local artist made good and bought a second-hand MGB, which allowed him to travel to galleries in a bit more style and also cut the journey time between Yorkshire and London, trips he was now making every week. He bought an art directory listing all the art galleries in and around the capital and spent months trawling round them with his portfolio to inquire about possible exhibition space. But this was costing him both time and money, and every day he spent in London meant he wasn't signwriting or painting:

> I was going down once a week and I was sleeping in Hyde Park in the back of my car. I'd wake up and go to Paddington Station for a wash and brush up and I'd put my suit on and call in on as many galleries as I could. Then I'd drive back home.

By the start of 1968 Anne was pregnant and they began looking for a bigger house. They had lived in their cramped terraced cottage for the past six years but it was far from ideal if they were going to raise a family. Ashley found a suitable semi-detached bungalow close by and managed to raise the required mortgage. But when Anne had to quit her job, as she had no maternity leave, they lost the cushion of her £18-a-week wage. It meant Ashley now had to pay all the bills on top of the increasing cost of buying art materials and travelling to and from the capital:

> There were some days I would work right up until midnight. I was still doing a lot of signwriting work, lettering vans, gable ends, even lavatory doors – anything that paid.

He piled even more pressure on their fragile financial situation by setting up a new studio and gallery. His old friend Mary Hayden told him that the small florists next door to her art shop had become available. It was £5 a week rent, but it was too good an opportunity to turn down. Anne feared they couldn't afford it but Ashley had already signed on the dotted line using the last of their savings. They opened with a flourish on the last day of August, attracting a batch of stories in the local press. It was the first ever professional art gallery in Barnsley and a triumphant moment for Ashley, who felt he had proved his critics wrong.

However, now he had to impress the art mandarins in London. He stepped up his visits to the capital and appeared to have made a breakthrough when one metropolitan gallery, impressed by all the publicity he was getting, invited him down so they could see his portfolio. But when he turned up the meeting was a disaster:

The minute I walked in I froze. Someone at the gallery had obviously made a mistake because the whole place was devoted to surrealism. The walls were covered with all sorts of weird paintings.

Still, he'd come this far he may as well show them his works:

The director came down and took one look at my portfolio and launched into a tirade about chocolate box painters and told me to 'get this crap' out of his gallery. So I grabbed my paintings and ran out.

He found the nearest phone box and rang Anne:

I broke down in tears and said I was finished. I told her what had happened, but she talked me round, not for the first time. She told me not to give up and I think if it hadn't been for her I would have thrown in the towel, because that was one of my lowest points.

He continued working hard to keep his family's financial head above water, but it seemed as though every avenue of opportunity turned into a dead end. The only cause for celebration was the birth of his first daughter, Heather, on November 11. Although his confidence had taken a knock he now had another, compelling reason to succeed. And, in any case, a new year was just around the corner.

Ashley and Anne with baby Heather.

# 7

# *Twist or Bust*

For many people 1969 was a defining moment. It was the year man first set foot on the moon, Richard Nixon took office in the White House and a hitherto unknown village called Woodstock wrote itself into the annals of pop history. It was also a pivotal one for Ashley, although it began with an unexpected, and precarious, trip to sea:

I've often said that, to me, the Yorkshire Moors and the Pennines are like frozen seas and I wanted to paint the real, moving seas, the only problem was I didn't know anybody who had a boat.

But a chance discussion led him to someone who did:

I was in my gallery one day and this girl came in who was going out with one of my pals from Barnsley. She was a bit of a hippie and we ended up sitting down on the floor talking about my work. I happened to mention in passing that one thing I really wanted to do was go out onto the high seas, at which point she said her father

Ashley with Danny La Rue at an exhibition at the Three Acres, Shelley.

One of the results of Ashley's adventures on board the *Conjuan*.

owned a fleet of trawlers up in the North East and told me she would have a word with him.

She kept her word and a couple of weeks later he was invited to join the eight-man crew of the *Conjuan*, a 70ft trawler that was heading out into the North Sea. He drove up to Newcastle and arrived at the South Shields docks but couldn't find the boat:

I said to a guy who was loading some cargo onto a ship, 'I'm looking for the *Conjuan*?' and he said, 'It's there,' and he pointed to the quayside but I couldn't see it. He told me to walk to the edge of the quay so I did and I looked down and there she was, although she didn't look much bigger than a fishing boat to me. I thought I was going out on one of those big trawlers.

Nevertheless, he jumped on board and spent the next three days at sea among the fishing grounds off the Icelandic coast:

We went out in the middle of winter to what's called the 'seaman's graveyard', the white sea. It was unbelievably cold. If you put your hands on the side of the railings your skin would come off.

Despite the freezing weather and suffering frequent bouts of seasickness, it was an invaluable experience:

It made me realize how hard it is for trawlermen to make a living. But I managed to do a load of sketches that I turned into paintings. And I learnt how to do what

I call these echoes, the circles of mist that I sometimes paint, from when I was sketching at sea.

Not long afterwards he lined up an exhibition in Dewsbury. This gave him the chance to sell a few more paintings, but as with all exhibitions it was a nerve-wracking experience:

It's difficult because you stand there on show trying to remember the names of the dignitaries and answering lots of questions. At the same time you're trying to hear what people are saying about your paintings and praying to God they pull out their chequebooks.

All these thoughts were racing through his head when he noticed a grey haired man out of the corner of his eye who he vaguely recognized. It was James L Brooke, a highly respected art critic and collector and a close friend of LS Lowry:

I knew he was an art expert and a brilliant art restorer and he came over to me and said, 'Ashley, I'm going to write to you because I like what you're doing.' I think I just stood there, I was lost for words.

A few days later Ashley received a letter from him:

He wrote that he had never met such a young watercolourist capable of painting in such broad, confident washes. He also admitted that he had tried for years to perfect the same technique without success.

Above all, he urged him to continue painting. It was the start of a friendship between the two men that lasted up until Brooke's death. His final act of kindness was to bequeath Lowry's palate to him, which he uses to this day.

Emboldened by Brooke's letter of praise, Ashley headed back down to London. Initially he was met by yet more rejections, but then one summer's day he entered the plush surroundings of the Upper Grosvenor Gallery, off Park Lane. As he walked in a couple of staff were gingerly taking down a Pietro Annigoni portrait and hanging a painting by the impressionist Dame Laura Knight. In the past Ashley would have simply done an about turn and walked out. But before he had time to do anything an elegant-looking young man wearing a green velvet suit had waltzed over and was asking if he could help.

I told him who I was and showed him my portfolio. He flicked through it without saying a word and then told me to leave it with him and he'd show it to the governors. 'Come back next week and I'll let you know their decision.'

Finally it seemed like he was making headway. But when he returned the gallery manager, who he'd been speaking to, told him the governors had been away and hadn't found time to look at his works, at which point Ashley lost his rag:

I felt I was being messed around and I told him, 'This is costing me money, I can't keep popping up and down all the time. If you don't think my paintings are good enough then at least have the decency to tell me.'

The gallery manager was apologetic and reassured him that his paintings were very good and that he would get back to him as soon as possible. Ashley drove back home disillusioned and still no nearer a breakthrough. But a few days later he received a telegram from the gallery saying: 'Ashley, congratulations, one-man exhibition in six weeks time, give us a call.'

He was ecstatic. He had a two-week exhibition in the heart of London. This was his first one-man exhibition in the capital and he was going to need to raise some cash if he was going to profit from it:

Because I was an artist we couldn't get a mortgage from any of the big banks, the only place we could get one was from the Yorkshire Penny Bank as it used to be called. I had to go cap in hand to my bank manager and sign our house away.

It was something he would be forced to do seven more times throughout his career, gambling his family's home on what Rudyard Kipling called 'one turn of pitch-and-toss'. He ended up borrowing the equivalent of £1,500, which was needed to pay for the brochures, mailing-list invitations, catalogues, transporting his paintings to and from the gallery and champagne for the launch party, among a host of other costs. The gallery also took thirty-three per cent of any sale which meant Ashley had to increase the cost of his paintings if he was going to make any profit. He marked up his paintings so those that would normally fetch fifty guineas increased to 120 (roughly £125 in today's money). But he was concerned that people wouldn't pay these inflated prices.

The Browns and Reds of the Moor – above Holme Valley.

Prior to the exhibition he travelled down to the gallery to meet the governors, including the Duchess of St Albans. She was the closest person to royalty he'd met in his life before, something he found a little unnerving:

I was a bit embarrassed because I didn't know how to address her, whether I should call her 'Your Grace,' or 'Ma'am'? But she laughed and said, 'Please just call me Suzanne, that's my name.'

The two of them walked round the gallery together to inspect the paintings as they were being hung, but then the Duchess stopped and shook her head:

I thought she was going to say they were too expensive, but she said, 'No, no, they're too cheap Ashley, you're under pricing yourself. Put them up.'

The price tags were quickly changed and for the first time an Ashley Jackson watercolour was being put up for sale at 150 guineas.

Ashley had spent many hours cultivating national and local press contacts in the watering holes of London and Yorkshire which he now used to great effect. The national newspapers dubbed him the 'Rain Man' and news of the exhibition appeared in the William Hickey column in the *Daily Express*, as well as *The Times*, the *Sun*, and the *Yorkshire Post*, while the *Barnsley Chronicle* deemed it worthy of a place on its front page. A couple of days before the exhibition launch he received a call from BBC's *Today* show inviting him to do an interview with Bill Grundy in Manchester. He agreed and visited his friend Elsie Robinson, one of the contributors to the William Hickey column, to see if she could give him any advice about interview etiquette:

It was the first time I'd done a radio interview and she said to me, 'Be careful with Bill Grundy, he can be a right bastard when he's interviewing.'

With this warning ringing in his head, he and Anne travelled across the Pennines:

Bill Grundy was there with his dark glasses on and he beckoned me into the studio and said, 'Ashley Jackson, Bill Grundy's my name, pleased to meet you.' And I said 'Pleased to meet you, sir.'

Ashley admitted to him that he was nervous because he'd heard he could be a difficult interviewer:

He just started laughing and said, 'Ashley I'll take you through it nice and steady.' So the interview started and he said, 'You've put your house on the line for this exhibition?' and I said, 'Yes, I believe in myself and my family'. He said, 'Well, you've got guts.' And through the whole interview he was great, he kept on plugging me as a young northern artist and I'm grateful for that.

It was during the interview with Grundy that he mentioned one of the reasons he was so desperate to be an artist:

He asked me what I wanted from painting and I said,

Ashley at his first exhibition in London, at the Upper Grosvenor Gallery with Bill Kenworthy, Derek Robinson and Rick Whiteley.

'Immortality,' and he almost fell out of his chair.

But think how many people carve their names into trees and why do they do that? It's the same with graffiti artists who spray their initials on walls, they're doing that because the world's passing them by and they just want to say, 'I'm here and no bugger's interested.'

He travelled down to London in high spirits. He had 30 paintings on display and by the time the exhibition came to a close a couple of weeks later he had sold ten of them. This was a considerable achievement for a young, relatively unknown artist enjoying his first exhibition in the capital. The critics, too, were kind, praising his bold, atmospheric paintings. It was the first of several exhibitions he was to have at the swanky Mayfair gallery, although it had been a big financial gamble:

We repaid the bank what we'd borrowed which was a big relief because otherwise we would have had to put our bungalow up for sale and move back into a rented cottage. By the time all the bills were totted up I just about broke even.

Ashley filming for a BBC omnibus programme in 1968.

But although the exhibition hadn't been a huge financial success, the publicity it gave him was priceless. He rang the Duchess of St Albans a week later to thank her for her support:

Someone picked up the phone and I said, 'Excuse me, are you the Duchess of St Albans' husband?' And the guy said, 'No, I'm the butler.' He told me that 'Madam' was not in, but 'Sir' was. He came on the line and I introduced myself and he told me that the Duchess was out so I gave him a message. I asked him if he'd ever been to Yorkshire and he said he hadn't. At the time I'd just bought a static caravan in Hawes that doubled up as a holiday home and a base that I could use to go sketching. So I said, 'If you ever fancy coming up you're welcome to stay in our caravan.' And I could just sense him putting his hand over the phone and saying to himself, 'Where the hell's she picked this one up from?'

What the London exhibition had taught him was that the number of paintings he sold was inextricably linked to the number of column inches in the newspapers. He had deliberately cultivated a string of press contacts and now he was slowly reaping the rewards. But while he had undeniably become adept at self-promotion and was now charging more for his works, he didn't want to price people out so he started producing smaller prints and watercolour sketches on cards that he sold for as little as four shillings:

I realized that if I was going to make a decent living from being an artist then there should be something for everyone. You can't just rely on selling your most expensive works once a blue moon to rich benefactors and expect to survive. It's the bread and butter stuff that counts and it's the average man in the street who's kept me in business.

The 1960s had proved to be a tumultuous decade for Ashley, but with a new one about to dawn there was one more surprise in store.

Sketch of Ashley's gallery in Dodworth.

# 8

# A Visit From the Matchstick Man

The American poet Carl Sandburg once noted that the best things in life are usually unexpected, and so it proved for Ashley on October 11, 1969. It had been an uneventful morning, a large part of which he had spent in his gallery workshop that had recently been extended into the neighbouring art shop:

I'd missed breakfast so I popped next door to get some remove chips. I was sitting in the studio having a sandwich when my assistant came in and told me that two gentlemen were here to see me. I told her I'd be with them in a minute and I think I was still munching on my sandwich when I came out and this guy introduced himself as Colonel Knowles.

He froze when he saw the second man. He was old and wore a long black coat the shoulders of which were sprinkled with dandruff. He had national health glasses, a dark trilby hat, a thin black tie and a starch white handkerchief jutted out from his top pocket. It was LS Lowry:

I recognized him immediately from photographs I'd seen

L S Lowry photographed by Dennis Thorpe.

and the first thing I said was, 'Mr Lowry, I feel as though Jesus Christ has just walked through the door.'

The famous, gaunt-looking figure looked at him and replied 'Nay lad, I'm only human'.

James L Brooke had taken Lowry to an exhibition of Ashley's work at the George Hotel, in Huddersfield, which impressed Lowry enough to make him want to meet the young watercolourist. Ashley was shocked that one of the greatest artists of the twentieth century had turned up at his gallery, but recovered his composure and pulled over a chair for Lowry to sit on:

I watched him silently as he looked around the room, wondering what he was going to say next.

Lowry spotted the display of art materials and decided to buy a sketchbook. Ashley tried to offer it to him as a gift but he refused, saying he couldn't afford to do things like that. He then began a closer inspection of the paintings displayed on the walls:

It was like waiting for a judge to pass sentence and then he said, 'I take my hat off to you, sir. Indeed, I will take it off to any good watercolourist, and you are one of the finest there is, sir. I only paint in oils, and that's easy compared with what you do. Mind, if you want some advice from me, I would tell you to give it up. No one should paint for a living. It's too painful. But if you intend to carry on, then keep doing the same thing.'

Lowry called everyone 'sir' but Ashley couldn't believe it was being addressed to him and further still he couldn't fully comprehend the praise being lavished on him by such a master craftsman. Lowry then announced he was going to buy one of the 'young man's paintings'. He chose a dark-hued impression entitled *Where Counties Meet*, a moorland scene of the border between Yorkshire, Lancashire and Derbyshire. Again Ashley offered it to him as a gift but again he refused and handed over ten guineas for the picture.

The pair sat and talked for a while and Ashley told him about his struggle to gain acceptance from London's fickle art establishment, to which Lowry replied, 'It was just the same for me, sir. Keep fighting, Ashley. Keep fighting if you mean to stick with it. They do not care for the likes of us down there. They used to laugh at my paintings, too. But they are not laughing now, are they sir?' Before he left, Lowry wrote down his address and telephone number and said he could call to see him any time if he wanted advice.

Two weeks later Ashley plucked up the courage to visit Lowry at his home in Mottram, on the outskirts of Manchester. He wasn't sure if he'd extended the offer to visit him out of politeness, or whether he really meant it. So he was understandably nervous as he knocked on his front door:

It reminded me of a prison because the door had at least six locks and a chain.

After what seemed like eternity the door creaked open and a voice snapped, 'Yes, who is it?' Ashley answered and after another long pause he was invited inside. He was led through a

When the Wind Blows, Cut Gate.

Ashley with his two daughters, Heather and Claudia. © Yorkshire Post.

dimly-lit corridor and into a sitting room that looked as though it hadn't changed since 1939, when Lowry's mother had died. Three well-worn chairs were positioned around a gas fire and a stack of paintings were piled against a wall. A large bowl full of unopened letters stood in the middle of a table:

I followed him in and remember thinking he must have smoked because his black jacket was covered with white specks and then I realized it was dandruff. He told me to take a seat and then he said, 'Why do you want to be friends with me?' And I said, 'Well Mr Lowry, I admire your works very much and I'm an artist and I'm proud to be sat in your company.' 'So you don't want anything from me?' And I said, 'No'.

The two men then sat and talked for several hours, after which Lowry showed him round the rest of his house. It was littered with antique clocks, which his mother had liked, and there was dust everywhere:

In the hallway you could see the old plaster where the wallpaper had fallen down and there were naked light bulbs dangling from the ceiling. Yet the art works he had hanging on his walls were priceless.

In his front room there were a couple of drawings by Leonardo Da Vinci and Michelangelo. He saw me looking at them and he said, 'The only other person to have any like it lives in Buckingham Palace.'

He even kept paintings beneath his bed. He had an original Canaletto under his bed bedside this gazunder and I asked him, 'My painting isn't under the bed is it, Mr Lowry?' Thankfully it wasn't.

Over the next six years Ashley visited Lowry a couple of times each month. Sometimes he would meet Lowry and Brooke for afternoon tea at the George Hotel, but usually he would drive across the Pennines to his home. Here they would talk about art and Lowry would give him advice about how to deal with critics, agents and gallery owners:

Lowry taught me a lot of things and he told me once, 'Never ask to join a society, because it gives them the chance to refuse you. Wait until they ask and then you have the right to refuse them. If anyone is going to make money out of your talent, then let it be you.'

As their friendship grew, Ashley started taking his two daughters along with him, Claudia having been born in September, 1970:

He liked children's company because they didn't want anything from him, whereas everybody else would pester him to draw something. He would often talk to me through Heather and Claudia, telling them what he thought I should do. They loved listening to him because he had a special aura that made each visit a memorable event.

I took Heather to see him one time when she was about six or seven. He asked her what she liked doing and she said reading. 'And what do you read?' 'Books'. And he burst out laughing, 'Well I will ask a stupid question.'

Ashley was able to tap into Lowry's vast experience, although when he asked him to criticize his paintings he refused:

Each one is trying to say something and that must be respected. So why should I criticize any artist's work?

Nevertheless, whenever Lowry did give him advice it was usually spot on, as it proved to be when Ashley was agonizing over which paintings to submit for a series of annual exhibitions one year:

I had a portfolio of new work that he agreed to look at, but I realized I'd included a painting I didn't think was good enough. I managed to press it against another one so that he turned over two at the same time. But he realized what I'd done and said, 'Why did you not want to show it to me, Ashley?' I explained why and he replied, 'But it's the best of the lot. Send it to the Royal Institute's next exhibition.' So I did and they accepted it.

Many of the stories Lowry regaled reflected his love of children, which Ashley had seen first hand in the way he treated Heather and Claudia:

He used to love going to the North East and on one visit he was trying to work out how best to paint a bridge. He said he spent half the day walking round this bridge trying to find the best angle and got nowhere. So he went for a walk in the centre of Newcastle and came across an exhibition of paintings by children and there was one of that bridge. He said, 'Ashley, it had everything in it that I was seeking to capture. It was so good that I gave up the idea of doing it myself. The artist was a girl and she was six years old.'

Such self-deprecation was not uncommon with Lowry:

I told him his style was unique and he said it wasn't and he went and fetched a book showing some works by the American artist Grandma Moses.

But the difference between Grandma Moses and Helen Bradley and all the other people who tried to copy Lowry was their matchstick people all go across the painting, Lowry's went in.

If you look at a Lowry painting you'll see a pathway in between people taking you into the picture. Lowry knew about perspective, he could draw beautifully well, he could do a portrait with a pencil that you would not believe.

Lowry was also a champion of aspiring artists who he believed had talent, irrespective of their social background:

He told me about a friend of his who worked as a toilet attendant and painted in his spare time and who was having an exhibition. Lowry's attitude was there's nothing wrong with being a lavatory attendant and that you didn't have to be an intellectual in order to be an artist.

Despite his acts of kindness and generosity, Ashley witnessed another side to Lowry's character:

He came across as an embittered man at times. He believed that society treated artists badly and he often repeated variations of the gloomy words he told me when we first met. 'You should never have become a painter, Ashley. It involves too much pain. It's not worth it.'

It's perhaps easy to forget that even the greatest artists suffer rejection during their careers and although Lowry enjoyed critical and commercial success during his own lifetime, Ashley believes the rejections he experienced when he was younger left an indelible mark on him:

He would say to me, 'When I started they scorned me. Now they want to give me honours. Well, they can keep them, sir.'

In his latter years, Lowry's public appearances became increasingly rare and Ashley was among the few people he allowed into his inner sanctum:

A couple of years before he died he invited me along to an exhibition of his work. When we arrived there was a bevy of pressmen waiting for him. One reporter asked him which his favourite painting was and Lowry looked at him and pointed with his walking stick to a glass box containing a fire extinguisher. Another guy asked the same question and he finally pointed to a small canvas on one of the walls. And when he was asked why he said, 'Because it was the first one I sold.' 'How much did you sell it for?' and he said fifteen guineas. Then the reporter

Ashley with his 'mistress'. © *Daily Mail*

asked, 'How much is worth now?' and he said around £20,000. 'How do you feel about that?' and Lowry looked at him and replied: 'I feel like a racehorse which has just won its first race.' That's what he was like, he had a very dry sense of humour and he didn't suffer fools.

One person who was particularly intrigued by Ashley's relationship with Lowry was Roy Mason. The Yorkshire MP was President of the Board of Trade when Ashley first met him and the two men had become close friends. Mason asked him if he could introduce him to Lowry, who he had long admired, which Ashley duly arranged.

I turned up at his house with Roy and his wife and he was quite charming. When he was in the right mood he loved to hold court and Roy was thrilled to meet him.

Mason even listened respectfully when Lowry launched an attack on the Government for not doing enough to protect artists. Once the political banter had finished the conversation moved towards less contentious topics and Lowry mentioned he was planning a trip to Sunderland. At which point Mason leaned over and whispered to Ashley, 'He's got himself a bird.' But Lowry overheard him and said, 'What is that you say, sir?' forcing Mason, in his best Parliamentary voice, to ask if he was going to see a lady.

'No sir, I have never had a young lady, and never has a young lady wanted me,' replied Lowry.

The Jackson family. © Yorkshire Post

This interminable sadness was something Ashley became increasingly aware of during Lowry's twilight years. And during one particular visit he found him almost inconsolable:

He said that all his old friends had gone. He told me that he'd been into the village that morning and found they were flying a flag half-mast over the working men's club for the last of them and he looked at me and said, 'I'm ready to go too, Ashley.'

He remembers their last conversation:

He said to me, 'If people are still talking about you thirty years after you died then you'll live forever.' And I think deep down he would be chuffed to bits that his work is still so popular.

During what proved to be their final meeting Lowry mentioned he was having a retrospective exhibition of his work at the Royal Academy and invited him along. But not long afterwards Ashley received a call from another of Lowry's close circle of friends telling him that he was in hospital suffering from pneumonia. He rang the hospital but was told the artist was too ill to see anyone. It was a few days later, while driving over the moors, that he heard on the radio that Lowry had died. He had barely returned home when Austin Mitchell, then one of Yorkshire Television's top presenters, rang asking him to come to the studio to reminisce about the great artist's life.

A few weeks later an engraved letter arrived in the post. It was an invitation from the Royal Academy's president to the official preview of Lowry's exhibition. He travelled down with

Heather, although he wondered what Lowry would have made of it all:

It was full of pompous, well-connected people, what I call the pseudo-intellectuals of the art world, most of whom didn't even know Lowry. As we walked in someone from one of the societies said, 'Ashley Jackson, what are you doing here?' and I said, 'Unlike you, I was invited by the man himself,' and he looked surprised and said, 'You knew Lowry?' and I said, 'Yes,' and walked off.

The exhibition proved a fitting tribute to Lowry, breaking all attendance records for a twentieth century artist. And for Ashley, it was the chance to pay homage to one of his heroes:

I've always said Turner is my god and Lowry is my mentor and it's been one of my greatest privileges to get to know such a great man.

# 9

# Behind Bars

By the late 1960s, Ashley was dividing his time between signwriting and painting. As well as holding watercolour demonstrations at art clubs and societies dotted around Yorkshire, he also taught evening classes to help supplement his income. But he now wanted a different challenge and approached the authorities at the notorious Wakefield Prison about the possibility of teaching art to the inmates there:

> I was a bit of a no-hoper at school and I wanted to work with prisoners, just as I still work with disadvantaged children today, because I've always felt that I could have very easily ended up in the same place. My saving grace was painting, that's what gave me a purpose in life.

After a meeting with the prison's education officer, Richard Brooks, it was agreed that he would hold three hour-long classes each week. He was made to sign the Official Secrets Act and within two weeks he started as a volunteer. He ran the classes for the next decade, although he admits that teaching in the country's largest maximum security jail was tough to begin with:

I'd never been in a prison before so it was a bit daunting when I first went in. The thing that hits you first is the smell from the 'slop out' as they used to call it. I

Ashley's art class at Wakefield Prison.

remember walking down the corridor on my first day and this guy gave me a crack as I walked past him, but I didn't say anything and two or three days later he came towards me and I thought 'Oh no, not again.' He stopped me and put his hand out and said, 'Welcome to Wakefield, Ashley, you're not a grasser.'

Having been accepted, at least by some of the inmates, he soon gained an understanding of the protocol of prison life:

I never asked them what they were inside for, all I wanted to do was to help them paint. Some of them were very good but most had no idea they could paint because no one had bothered to teach them before. They started by copying photographs of their wives and children on to pieces of hardboard and showed them to their partners when they came to visit. There was one guy from the East End of London who did these beautiful paintings of big men and women sitting on their doorsteps. They reminded me of Rubens' work they were that good.

Although there was a shortage of art materials in jail, he found a way round this by collecting old brushes and pencils from local art groups and taking them in for the prisoners to use. To begin with the inmates were reluctant to pick up a brush or a pencil and those that did attend the classes came to listen, not to paint. But gradually more and more became involved, painting everything from portraits and landscapes, to sketches, oils and watercolours:

When we did still life classes I would ask them what fruit they wanted me to bring and they'd ask for some melons, so I'd take some in for them to draw and afterwards they'd eat them.

They painted murals for the rooms in the jail and even painted one for the prison officers' club. Within just twelve months there was a three-year waiting list to join his art class. Several members of the group won Koestler Awards, set up by Arthur Koestler to encourage prisoners to take up painting, which led to a TV documentary for the BBC's Omnibus programme featuring Ashley and his class.

Over the years he found himself forming friendships with some of the inmates, which perhaps isn't surprising given the fact he was seeing them week in and week out:

There was one lad who was a brilliant artist, he did these Red Indian scenes and we got talking one day. He was in his twenties and he told me that he got into trouble when he was fourteen. He got into a fight with this kid and stabbed him with a penknife and the lad died. He'd already done a long stretch by the time I met him and although he had committed a terrible crime, I felt for him.

He mentioned the case to Roy Mason who passed it on to the Home Secretary and eventually the man was released on license:

Not long afterwards his mother and father came to see me in my gallery. They both started weeping, they told me they were looking after him but said he spent most of his time lying in bed staring at the ceiling. And I explained to them that he'd been doing this for the last fourteen years. Because that's what you do if you're locked up, you go off into a world of your own.

I used to see him from time to time and whenever I was doing my talks and demonstrations in Yorkshire he would sit at the back listening. I lost contact with him about twenty years ago but I think about him from time to time. I just hope he didn't end up back inside.

Teaching prisoners also made him appreciate his own life and family all the more:

I remember we had just finished a class and this guy asked me what I was going to do the next day and I told him I was going out on the moors to paint, and he said: 'Ash, I can only see the hills in the distance when I stand on a chair and look out the jam jar window. When you go up there could you shout out my name and come back and tell me what you've seen?'

It stopped me in my tracks, he knew he might not ever be up on the moors again and it made me think that life's too short, which is why I try and seize the day because I don't want to end up lying on my deathbed thinking I should have done more with my time.

Even though he was teaching criminals, some of who were convicted murderers, there was the odd occasion when he helped them out, even if it meant bending the rules:

One of Ashley's art classes at Wakefield Prison where he taught for more than a decade.

There was a guy I'd become friendly with who came to my classes and one day he was really down. He told me his daughter had MS and that she was dying. He said he was going to wreck the place because he'd been told he could go to the funeral but he couldn't go and see her to say goodbye. I persuaded him not to do anything rash and I asked him to give me the name of the hospital she was in and I'd go and see her for him.

He travelled to St James's Hospital, in Leeds, where she was a patient:

The nurses said only close friends and family were allowed to see her, so I said I'd been a friend of her father's for years, which was true. There were twelve beds on the ward but I suddenly realized I had no idea what she looked like and it was pure luck that I went to the right bed. I said to her, 'You don't know who I am,' but she said she did because her father had mentioned I was coming. I gave her the message he'd asked me to give her and we both cried. Then I gave her a hug and said, 'That's from your dad'.

That evening he arrived at the prison for his art class and had barely set foot inside when he was quizzed by his boss about where he'd been:

Teaching in Wakefield Prison with Don Booker, left, former editor of the Barnsley Chronicle.

I told the truth. I explained that I'd been to Jimmy's and I told him why and he told me not to do it again.

Ashley was also involved in what must rank as one of the most unusual nights in the prison's history. He had always made a point of promoting the prisoners' work, even helping to arrange an exhibition of their paintings at the *Yorkshire Post*'s head office in Leeds. Then out of the blue he got a call from his uncle Clive, who was now a musician. He was touring the north of England with his Norwegian country and western band, which happened to be the opening act for Freddie Starr. At the time, Starr was one of the hottest young acts around and Ashley asked Clive to see if the comedian would come and do a gig for the prisoners at Wakefield Prison, à la Johnny Cash at San Quentin. Much to his surprise the comic agreed:

Most of the prisoners were there and so, too, were the officers. The assistant governor even brought his son along and they sat on the front row.

Well, Freddie was playing to the audience, he was swearing and doing his impersonations and by the time he finished the lads were all cheering and dancing in the aisles.

But not everyone enjoyed the show:

The assistant governor said it was an absolute disgrace because of all the bad language in front of his son. But what did he expect at a gig to a crowd full of criminals?

Of all the inmates he taught at Wakefield Prison, Michael Luvaglio was the most well-known. Luvaglio, along with Dennis Stafford, had been convicted of killing a fruit machine cash collector in what became known as the 'One-Armed Bandit Murder', which inspired the film *Get Carter*, starring Michael Caine. Over the years Ashley got to know Luvaglio reasonably well:

He was quiet but he seemed like a nice guy, he used to make miniature caravans and he even made one for my children.

Luvaglio had protested his innocence ever since his conviction but he had two appeals turned down before he was eventually freed in 1979 on license. However, Ashley found himself roped into the case. He had been teaching as normal one evening when a prison officer interrupted his class, telling him there was a telephone call for him:

I followed him into one of the offices and picked up the receiver and this guy said, 'It's in connection with Michael Luvaglio'. My first reaction was, 'Had I done something wrong?' but as he was talking I heard voices in the background and I said, 'Are those my children I can hear?' and he said, 'Yes, I'm at your house'. I was trying not to panic, so I arranged to meet him in a car park outside the prison.

His wife Anne had been at home with the children when the stranger turned up asking to speak to her husband. 'I told him that Ashley was teaching and without thinking I invited him inside so he could ring the prison.'

Meanwhile, Ashley finished his class and told the governor what had happened.

He said he knew about the call and that it was ok. So I went across the road and met this guy who wanted to subpoena me to go to the high court as a character witness for Luvaglio's appeal. I told him he didn't have to subpoena me because I'd do it.

He travelled down to the Court of Appeal, which rejected Luvaglio's case. But a few weeks after the hearing he was on his way to his art class when one of the inmates came over and quizzed him about why he had gone down to London:

They thought I'd gone down in support of the authorities and not Luvaglio and he told me there was a job out to scold me, because that's what happened if you did the dirty on someone.

Not long after this he decided to call it a day:

I just felt that I'd done my bit and I didn't want the inmates thinking I was helping the prison authorities, because that wasn't why I was there.

Hade Edge near Holmfirth with Castle Hill in the distance.

88

Despite this incident teaching at Wakefield gave him a rare insight to prisoners' lives:

The prison officers will tell you that those who've become institutionalized don't have any trouble with prison because when that bell goes they go to their cells, just like they've been doing their whole adult life.

A lot of people who end up in prison come from broken homes, or the wrong side of the tracks. They get shunted from home to home, some are beaten or abused, and they start thinking, 'Nobody gives a damn about me'. Then they do something wrong and wind up in borstal and when that happens they're on a downward spiral, and more often than not they end up in prison."

But Ashley found that many of the inmates he taught showed a natural aptitude for painting:

Most of them haven't been given a proper chance to show an interest in art or literature until they get into prison and because they can't do anything else, it just oozes out of them and they find skills they never realized they had. I'm not saying all prisoners are good people at heart, because most of them are there for a reason. But I never judged them, I treated them as equals.

His sympathetic attitude may surprise some people, but it goes back to his own troubled upbringing:

Ashley with the former governor of Wakefield Prison, John Watson, at an exhibition of art by the inmates – held at the Yorkshire Post Offices in Leeds.

My stepfather didn't know how heavy his hands were when he punched me, or how it made me feel. So I think that's one of the reasons I wanted to teach prisoners, because I knew where some of them had come from.

I looked at some of the inmates and thought, 'there but for the grace of God go I.' My father died when I was a child and I could have fallen in with the wrong crowd, but I was fortunate enough not to.

Roman Road Wheeldale Moor.

A photo of Ashley by Dennis Thorpe of the *Daily Mail* at Wuthering Heights, Top Withens, 1968.

# 10

# There's No Such Thing as a Free Lunch

As well as signwriting and teaching, Ashley spent many windswept hours up on the moors tirelessly honing his watercolour technique. If he was going to sell himself as a successful Yorkshire artist then he needed the works to back up his claims. He also strived to keep his name in the public eye, something he had achieved with no small amount of skill almost from the moment he held his first event in Brighouse. But if the Calder Valley town exhibit had helped get his fledgling career off the ground, it was in Barnsley that it had taken flight. Among the local politicians who had become his friends were Jack Brown, a writer and activist, and Ron Fisher, a respected town councillor. But there was another, far more prominent political figure who was to have the greatest influence on Ashley's career outside his family, Roy Mason.

Born in Royston, near Barnsley, Mason went on to have an extraordinary career. He began working in the Wharncliffe Woodmoor pits at the tender age of fourteen. He remained in the coal industry until he became Barnsley MP after winning a by-election in 1953. The short, pipe-smoking former miner quickly gained a formidable reputation within the Labour Party for his energy and tenacity. During the 1960s he was Labour's

Roy Mason visiting the Mall Gallery exhibition.

Ashley with Roy Mason, then President of the Board of Trade.

spokesman on Home Affairs and served in the Ministry of Power, before becoming President of the Board of Trade in 1969, the year he first met Ashley. It was Brown, a long-standing friend of Mason's, who introduced the pair:

> He said one day that he was meeting Roy Mason for a drink and that I ought to come down too, so I did.

They met at the Queens Hotel, in Barnsley:

> We chatted, he was drinking his whisky and I was drinking mine and he said, 'This could be more important

to you than me lad,' and handed me a box. He explained that he'd just been to Slazengers, which had a factory in Barnsley at the time. So I opened the box and inside were a load of Jumping Jacks condoms he'd been given.

The two men soon became friends and Ashley joined his informal drinking club, which included Brown, Fisher and *Financial Times* journalist Ron Kershaw:

> Mason could see that I needed publicity, as did he. So whenever big-name Yorkshire politicians were retiring he'd ask me to do paintings for them. I never got paid but it was good PR and it was a good way of getting in the local papers.

It was a mutually beneficial arrangement. Ashley got the publicity he needed to keep himself in the public eye, which, in turn, helped sell more paintings; while in return he gave Mason numerous paintings and drawings. Critics called it a marriage of convenience and Sir Marcus Fox, the former Conservative MP for Shipley, jokingly referred to Mason as Ashley's agent.

> People will say in the early days that he helped me, but we helped one another, it was a good partnership.

For Ashley, Mason was like a 'blood brother' and the fatherly mentor he never had:

> There's been two father figures my life. One was Ron Darwent and the other was Roy Mason, I would have done anything for him.

Storm on its way – Pennine Way.

Ashley with Prime Minister Harold Wilson at 10 Downing Street.

We were ushered inside and I thought we'd be kept waiting, but I couldn't believe it when Harold Wilson came bounding down the staircase and said, 'Hello Ashley, come on up.' So we walked into his private office and Mason was already there. There was a big painting of Lowry's on the wall and the Prime Minister said to me, 'I believe you know the man who painted that,' and I said, 'Yes, sir, I know him very well.' And he turned to me and said, 'He's a funny fella that Lowry. Do you know I offered him a knighthood and he turned me down, then I offered him the Companion of Honour and he refused that, too.' Just as he said that I went down on one knee as a joke and said, 'You could always give it to me instead.' But Mason said, 'Get up you silly bugger, it's the Prime Minister of Great Britain you're talking to.' I told Lowry the story not long afterwards and he burst out laughing.

Like many others, though, Ashley was hugely impressed by the Huddersfield-born politician:

Harold Wilson was a lovely man and you could tell that he had a razor-sharp brain. I told him that I'd started off in Milnsbridge and that I'd been a bugler in the Milnsbridge Baptist scouts and he said he was, too. He asked me what patrol I was in, and I said I was head of Cuckoo Patrol and it turned out that he was too, and then he leaned over and said, 'Don't let this get out, otherwise we'll look like a right couple of cuckoos.'

Ashley's close relationship with Mason gave him a rare glimpse into the Machiavellian world of government politics

Their friendship blossomed and he and Anne were often invited down to the House of Commons as Mason's guest. By the mid-70s the Barnsley MP was Defence Secretary and a pivotal figure in Harold Wilson's government. A few weeks after Ashley had introduced him to Lowry, Mason returned the favour by arranging for him to meet the Prime Minister at Downing Street:

Anne and I were picked up from our hotel in one of the Prime Minister's official cars with a flag flying on the bonnet and we were taken to Number 10.

and he remembers when Mason was made Secretary of State for Northern Ireland:

We were having a drink and he said to me, 'Ashley, you've got to be careful how you talk to the press.' He'd been asked by a reporter that if he was Northern Ireland secretary how would he do the job, so he gave him an answer which was then reported in all the big newspapers. He told me that Harold Wilson had called him in and played holy hell for making a comment.

Not long afterwards I met him for lunch at the Strangers' Bar in the House of Commons, and he said, 'Bloody hell, that bastard's given me Northern Ireland.' And as he said it a voice from the table behind said, 'I'll have half a fed', Roy' and we turned round and it was Harold Wilson.

Mason is regarded by many as the best Northern Ireland Secretary Britain has ever had and his uncompromising attitude towards the IRA earned him the nickname 'Stone Mason'. At the height of the Troubles he invited Ashley over to Belfast, having arranged a commission for him to paint the Short Brothers' aviation factory where they made jet planes. It was Ashley's first visit to Northern Ireland and it turned out to be an unpleasant one:

I was picked up at the airport in a chauffeur-driven car but I was shocked at what I saw. We drove past

Ashley and Mason share a joke with the Dodworth Brass band during the artist's exhibition at Foyles, in London.

roadblocks, burning buses and kids throwing rocks on our way to this secluded hotel out in the country.

That evening Mason hosted a special dinner, although Ashley found the whole atmosphere unnerving.

Mason arrived in a black Jaguar with what seemed like half an army. Two men with Sten guns stood at the entrance and there were dozens more guarding the place, you couldn't even go to the gents without staring down the barrel of a gun.

He was so worried about an IRA attack that when he went to bed he pushed a wardrobe behind his door. To cap it all off, the aviation firm didn't like the painting he did for them:

It had a jet flying over the factory, with a roadblock of oil drums in the foreground. But they said it created the wrong image and would put off their American customers, so I ended up doing a softer version with the Mourne Mountains in the background and I gave the original to Mason.

Their friendship continued over the years and in 1980 Mason told the *Yorkshire Post* of his admiration for Ashley, saying: 'He has probably put on the artists' map of Britain more of the Yorkshire moorland than any other artist I have ever known and I think this is worthy of encouragement.'

However, cracks were beginning to appear in their relationship:

His wife Marjorie bought a painting of Bill o' Jacks from me as a surprise anniversary present. But he came and had a right go at me. 'You rotten bugger,' he said, 'I'd have thought you would have given her that.' I tried to explain that I couldn't afford to give it away because it was one of my strongest paintings, but he wasn't interested.

Another incident strained matters further. Since the mid-80s, Ashley had helped raise money for the Prince's Trust and had been chairman of its Yorkshire Appeals board. He was asked by John Purvin, chief executive of the Prince's Youth Business Trust, if he would become chairman of the newly formed South Yorkshire region of Trust, which was dividing its Yorkshire operation into four parts. But Ashley declined because he felt it was time to hand over the reins to someone else:

I didn't want to be chairman but I told him that I knew Roy Mason and he would make a good chairman. So they approached him and he agreed, and to this day I don't think he knows that I put a good word in for him.

At the same time Ashley was putting the finishing touches to a new book, *Painting in the Open Air*.

A client of mine had some of my paintings including one of Marrick Priory and I told him I was bringing out this book and that this was the painting I wanted to use on the front cover. I held copyright anyway, but I wanted to tell him because we were friends.

The book was duly published but Ashley claims that Mason then became involved:

He apparently told my client that he held the copyright of this painting and advised him to sue me. We had to get a solicitor from The Prince's Trust to write to my client and explain that I had the copyright. I'd just helped to get him this role with the Trust and he turned round and did this, I couldn't believe it.

The artist presenting one of his works to Mason.

The final nail in the coffin came a short time later. Since the early 70s Ashley had created a series of specially-designed Christmas cards for Mason, who sent them to close family, friends and high-ranking dignitaries. Every year he made up to 100 of these cards, each featuring a different hand-painted landscape:

I didn't get paid for doing it, but these cards were sent to the Queen, the Prime Minister and other bigwigs. So

although it was very time-consuming it was a way of getting a bit of publicity. But it reached the stage where it was getting too difficult. So I met him for a drink and I said, 'I'm sorry Roy, I can't do your cards this year.' There was a recession on at the time and I was treading water and I asked him if he could get someone else to do them. He looked at me and said: 'Well then lad, I'll make sure as long as I live you never get a gong' – and that was that.

The artist during the presentation of his sketch of HMS *Sheffield,* with Patrick Duffy, Mason and the Barnsley Sea Cadets.

However, Ashley is not the only person who has felt let down by Mason. Sir Patrick Duffy, former MP for Sheffield Attercliffe and Under Secretary of State for the Royal Navy in Jim Callaghan's government, has been a colleague and close friend of Mason's for many years. In the early 90s, Duffy had been told by Cledwyn Hughes, then Labour Leader in the House of Lords, that he was among those shortlisted for a peerage. But after hearing nothing he sought the advice of his old friend, Mason:

To my surprise Roy repeatedly evaded attempts at such a meeting. I did catch him one morning, however, in the lower half of the Members' tea room, around 9am over coffee. That is how clear my recollection remains of the exchange, as well as Roy's refusal to assist, as he pointed out that without a privy councillorship I was not qualified.

Duffy had the support of Roy Hattersley and John Smith, but it was Mason who was putting a spoke in the wheels. After a lifetime's service to both the Labour Party and his country Duffy missed out on a peerage, largely, it seems, because of Mason's opposition. Despite this slap in the face he says he remained loyal to Mason, 'Even as I observed a Labour government shovelling all manner of people into the Lords, irrespective of service and credentials.'

Ashley confirms Duffy's story through a conversation he had with Mason, in which he stated that the Lord Chamberlain had contacted him about elevating Duffy to the Upper House but Mason had told him that a knighthood would be sufficient.

It is more than a decade since Ashley last spoke to Mason and despite the fact he has given him dozens of paintings and drawings over the years, he says he doesn't harbour a grudge:

I get on well with his wife, she's a lovely person, and so are his children. He did open doors for me and I'm very grateful for that, it's just sad that everything went sour. Anne once said that Roy Mason would make a good enemy if I ever fell out with him and she was right.

The George Inn – Hubberholme.

# 11

# Moving up in the World

Ever since returning with a handful of wobbly sketches from his stormy trip on the *Conjuan*, Ashley had been itching to go back out to sea. And it wasn't long before he was. Through his friendship with Mason he was commissioned by the MOD to paint various Royal Navy ships. His first naval job was painting HMS *Hermione*, a Leander-class frigate. He asked to paint the ship during winter to enable him to develop his appreciation of the vast swell of the Pennines, so it was arranged for him to join the crew in November. He reported to HMS *Hermione* at her berth in Liverpool where he was met by the captain and given the admiral's quarters. Before leaving port he was invited to go ashore as it would be his last chance for a couple of weeks. So he and four sailors went for night out in the city:

I thought we were going to a few bars but we ended up at this sauna and massage parlour and I thought, 'Ok, when in Rome.' It was staffed by young women and I'd never seen anything like it before. I'd only met these lads a few hours earlier and here we were sitting stark naked in a sauna room.

Once in a while we'd go and jump into this pool of ice-cold water and then one by one the lads went off to have a massage. Eventually one of the girls called out my name and beckoned me into a cubicle. I'm a happily married man but I couldn't really walk out so I went in and lay down on the bed. By this time I was feeling more than a little embarrassed realising that my equipment looked like a sparrow perched on two rocks after being in the cold water. I tried to cover myself with a towel but she pulled it away and told me to lie on my back. It was like being at the dentist so I closed my eyes and turned over, but when I opened them there were four faces peering over the top of my cubicle laughing. They'd set me up.

After getting dressed they were picked up by the admiral of the fleet's car and whisked back to the ship. Ashley spent the next two weeks at sea doing sketches and then returned home to complete the painting.

A month later he was invited to an official presentation ceremony of the painting. But to his surprise he was flown out by the RAF to join up with HMS *Hermione*'s crew in Gibraltar, where the ship was with the NATO fleet on exercise. Admiral Sir Terence Lewin, then Commander-in-Chief of the fleet and later First Sea Lord, flew in especially to make the presentation. The painting was unveiled accompanied by the sound of pipes and bugles on the quarterdeck and then Ashley was invited to have lunch with the Navy's top brass:

It was a nerve-wracking experience because it was just me and five admirals. Sir Terence raised a toast to me and then he said, 'Ashley, could you tell the admirals here what your shore leave was like in Liverpool, I hear you had a good time,' and they all started laughing, it seems half the fleet had heard about our visit to the massage parlour.

HMS *Fife*, a County-class destroyer, was another naval ship he was commissioned to paint. Again he was invited to an official unveiling ceremony, this time in Liverpool. It was followed by a lunch for high-ranking Royal Naval officers and their wives, a handful of local dignitaries, including the mayors of Liverpool and Birkenhead, and the artist himself:

The woman sitting next to me was the Rear-Admiral's wife. She was very posh and full of herself and she turned to me and said, 'So what are you doing on board ship?' If someone talks in a posh voice I tend to go broad, so I said, 'I'm the lad who painted the ship.' 'Oh, you're the painter chappie.' Well, that bloody riled me. Several other people on the table were suddenly tuned in to my conversation, sensing something was going to happen. So I said to this woman, 'Are you the Rear-Admiral's wife?'

and she said, 'Yes, how did you know he was a Rear-Admiral?' 'Because we're his guests and I noticed the cross of St George and a single red ball on his flag. Vice-Admirals have two and your husband's only got one red ball hasn't he?' Well, you can imagine how that went down. But one of the mayors picked up the baton and as we were being escorted off the ship he looked back at the ship's flag and said, 'He's right is Ash, he has only got one red ball.'

Among his numerous maritime commissions Ashley painted several submarines which presented their own, unique challenges:

I was about to start painting this particular nuclear submarine when a naval officer came up to me and said: 'Ashley, you know many people have tried painting submarines but it's not as easy as it looks. There's not much shape to them and quite often they end up looking like giant, floating turds.' So the whole time I was working on the painting I kept checking to make sure it didn't look like a turd moving through the water.

But of all his Royal Navy paintings the most poignant was HMS *Sheffield*. He went to sea to paint the guided missile destroyer during Sir Patrick Duffy's tenure as Navy Minister and the subsequent portrait was presented to the city of Sheffield. A few years later HMS *Sheffield* became the first major British casualty of the Falklands conflict when it was sunk with the loss of twenty lives. Ashley's painting still has pride of place in the city's town hall, where it has become a lasting tribute to those who died and a sober reminder of the vagaries of war.

Ashley on the moors with Barry Cockcroft, producer of *My Own Flesh and Blood*.

During the 1970s as his reputation grew, the jobs started rolling in, including commissions from people like Tony Christie and Geoffrey Boycott. His work also brought him into contact with the world of TV. By this time Yorkshire Television was attracting a growing band of talented programme makers, writers and directors, and Ashley was a regular visitor to its Leeds studios, becoming friends with people like Graham Ironside, Barry Cockcroft and Sid Waddell, the Geordie sports commentator. It was Waddell who helped Ashley land one of his more unusual jobs:

We were in the bar one day with he said, 'You fancy yourself as an artist, there's a job that might interest you.'

The job in question was to draw sketches for a TV political debate involving four Yorkshire MPs; Denis Healey, Roy Mason, Merlyn Rees and Marcus Fox:

I'm not a portrait painter but they must have been ok, because when the Poulson affair erupted I got a call from YTV who asked me to be their court artist for the trial in Leeds.

The Poulson in question was the infamous architect John Poulson, who was jailed in 1974 for five years after being found guilty of bribing public figures to win contracts.

By now Ashley was arguably the most well known artist living and working in the north of England and it wasn't long before he was sketching in front of the cameras. He was invited to appear on a late night culture show called *People To People* on BBC 2, along with TV presenter Donny MacLeod, scriptwriter Johnny Speight and Janet Street-Porter. The programme revolved around a north versus south debate and went out live with Ashley and MacLeod representing the north, and Speight and Street-Porter supporting the south:

Warm Rain – Black Hill, Holme Moss.

Janet Street Porter started off by saying people could be arrogant in the north and then the conversation moved on to culture and people's aspirations, and I happened to say if you wanted to see some of the poorest areas then go to Scotland, where you could still find people living under corrugated iron roofs.

Afterwards MacLeod came over and thanked him for his comments and asked if he might be interested in appearing on *Pebble Mill at One*, a popular afternoon chat show that became a British TV institution:

The programme went out live and the next day I got a phone call from a researcher at Pebble Mill saying they wanted to come up and have a look at my studio in Barnsley.

The show's producer, Terry Dobson, travelled to his gallery and after a quick inspection of his work said he wanted him to do a one-off, six-minute slot teaching kids how to paint. Ashley agreed and the following week he travelled down to the Pebble Mill studios in Birmingham:

I went into the studio garden with six or seven children looking out over trees and parked cars. It was cold and they all had their easels and I told them to follow what I did. But I said, 'Don't put the cars in, just draw the trees,' and this one kid said, 'Why not, mister?' and I said, 'Because I can't draw cars and you'll show me up.'

Afterwards Dobson congratulated him for his natural performance on camera:

He walked over to me puffing away on a cigarette and he said, 'Well done Ashley, that was great, give me another six programmes… no, make that fourteen, in fact make it twenty-three.'

His *How to Paint* slot became a regular feature of the show and he ended up doing a total of forty-eight shows in 1978 and then again in 1985:

It was great, I'd travel down on Sunday and the BBC would put me up in a hotel and I'd be there staying in Cliff Richard's suite, I couldn't believe it.

On each show he demonstrated different painting and drawing techniques:

It taught me how to paint for the cameras, because it was live and there was no room for waffling.

This national TV exposure week in, and week out, opened up a whole new audience to his work. But even with this and the fees he received from the BBC, the costs involved in staging exhibitions meant he still needed to accept signwriting jobs that came his way:

There were several occasions I'd be working on a shop front and someone would look up at me and say, 'Hey lad, I've just seen thee on the telly, what the hell are you doing up that ladder?' Everyone assumed that I'd made it, but I still had to work hard like everyone else.

However, this daily grind contrasted with some of the art commissions he was offered involving all expenses paid trips to private estates up and down the British Isles. His growing artistic reputation was also extending beyond our shores. He held a one-man exhibition at the Mall Gallery, in London, featuring paintings of the Iberian peninsula following a trip to Spain. Among those who attended the exhibition was Arthur Scargill, then president of the Yorkshire region of the NUM, who presented the Soviet ambassador and a group of visiting Russian mineworkers with a pit painting Ashley had done. Also there was the Spanish ambassador Fraga Iribarne, who briefly became Spain's vice-president and Interior Minister following the death of General Franco:

They were two political bulldogs you didn't put together. This was during the three-day week and the gallery was

in darkness for quite a while. So the Soviet ambassador came in the morning and Scargill presented him with a painting of the Yorkshire pits and in the afternoon the Spanish ambassador came.

Soon afterwards Ashley held an exhibition at the Spanish Institute of Culture, in London, which was followed by an invitation from Iribarne to take part in an exhibition on Lanzarote, as one of four Spanish artists. The invitation was extended to him because of his paternal grandmother's Spanish roots. The three other artists were Salvador Dali, Joan Miro and Pablo Picasso:

We each exhibited one painting, mine was of Langsett Moor and it was just unbelievable having my work alongside such brilliant artists.

By the end of the decade Ashley's paintings were being advertised in newspapers as potential investments. Works that ten years earlier were selling for £20 were now going for £600, while his most expensive paintings were fetching two, or even three thousand pounds. But although some wealthy clients had helped bump up his prices, it wasn't all about money:

A young couple came into my gallery one day to have a look at a painting they had seen in an exhibition at the Yorkshire Post offices. It was a moorland scene in winter and I'd priced it at a thousand pounds because I didn't really want to sell it. They left but the next day the guy rang up and asked if it was still for sale. I told him it was and he came over on his motorbike and put down £20 as a deposit. He wanted the painting as a surprise wedding anniversary present and he came back a week later with two cheques for the amount still owed, one from his bank and the other from a building society. Anne was looking after the gallery when he arrived but when she asked how he was going to carry it back on his bike, he told her that he'd come on the bus because he'd sold his bike to help pay for the painting.

I was back home and Anne rang me and said, 'Ashley I want you to speak to this man, he's sold his bike to buy a painting.' She put him on the phone and I said, 'Without meaning to sound rude, how did you get the money?' And he told me that he'd sold his bike so he could buy the painting. So I said, 'What does five hundred quid look like to you?' And he said, 'Why?' and I said, 'You can have the painting for five hundred quid.' And he burst into tears because it meant he could buy his bike back. It may have cost me, but when an ordinary working man makes a sacrifice like that to buy one of my paintings it means more than all the critics opinions put together.

Snowstorm, The Lion Inn, North Yorkshire.

# 12

# Who the Hell Am I?

As he approached his fortieth birthday Ashley appeared to have everything he had dreamed of. He had a loving wife and family, a big house nestled in the hills above Holmfirth and had established himself as an internationally renowned artist whose works adorned the walls of foreign embassies, Royal houses and the homes of the rich and famous. But there was something that had long niggled him – the question of who he was and where he came from:

Even though I never knew my father, I've always felt close to him somehow. That probably sounds strange given the fact I never spoke to him, but it's a feeling I've always had.

For years he had pored over the handful of grainy black and white photographs of his father that still existed, imagining what kind of man he was. It was this that slowly triggered his own identity crisis and fuelled a burning desire to learn more about his roots:

Most people take these kind of things for granted, they know who their parents are and where they come from, they know who their grandparents and even their great-grandparents were. But I had a lot of unanswered questions.

His mother didn't know much about his father's background other than the fact that his mother was Spanish and his father was either English, or American. The only other person who had been close to Ashley's father was his grandmother, Dolores Jackson, but she had been dead nearly twenty years. Nevertheless she held the key to the information he was after.

The summer trips to visit his grandmother in Limerick are among the few happy memories Ashley has of his early teenage years. It was during these visits that she regaled him with tales of her colourful life:

She told me how she had been a celebrated flamenco dancer when she was younger and travelled all over the world and even performed for Queen Victoria.

In Spain filming *My Own Flesh and Blood*.

He was entranced by these exotic stories as a youngster but he knew little about her childhood. She mentioned that she'd been born in Seville and that her maiden name meant 'king' in Spanish. He knew that her father had died when she was a young girl and that her mother had remarried. She also told him that when she was six she had been sold to an American couple who ran a troupe of travelling dancers, who had taken her to London. At the time he hadn't realized the significance of the word 'sold', it was only years later that it helped piece the jigsaw together.

It was Anne who eventually told him to take a break from work in order to try and find the answers to the questions plaguing him. But where should he begin such a mammoth odyssey? It was then that he remembered a little red book his grandmother bequeathed to him in her will. It was full of yellowing photographs and dusty press cuttings. He had flicked through the book many times before and regarded it as a precious memento. But now he re-read it, scrutinizing every page in the hope that it might shed some light on his clouded past. It was at this point that he stumbled on a strand of information that left him baffled. In a five-line paragraph about his grandmother's divorce taken from a fading copy of the *Singapore Straits Times*, he noticed a strange name pasted in a corner of the book, one he hadn't come across before. His grandmother's name read Dolores Rodriguez Jackson. It was the middle name that puzzled him:

I'd never heard that name before and I didn't know where it came from. I knew it didn't mean 'king' in Spanish, that was *Rey*. So I went and found a copy of her death certificate, but this had her down as Dolores

Jackson, which is the name I always knew. So it was back to square one.

The only other snippet of information he had was that she had married in London, so he travelled to the capital hoping to find some answers. Finally, after spending several days leafing through church registers he found what he was after. But the bride's name was listed as Maria Therese Rodriguez, daughter of Manuel Rodriguez, a 'gentleman farmer' from Seville. He checked the name again, but it was definitely his grandmother because she had married Theodore Stanley Jackson. He returned home deflated and even more confused than when he started. He quizzed his mother and his maternal grandmother, but they were equally surprised by this revelation.

He travelled back to Limerick for the first time since visiting his grandmother on her deathbed. He went to see his Aunt Mamie, who had been one of her closest friends, but she, too, was equally perplexed. Having reached a dead end here he decided to travel to Spain to try and unravel the mystery surrounding his grandmother's roots, and in doing so his own. He mentioned his plan over a few drinks one evening to Barry Cockcroft who suggested doing a TV programme following him as he traced his family tree. Cockcroft's award-winning documentary *Too Long A Winter* had made Hannah Hauxwell a household name and he and Ashley had been close friends for many years:

I was dubious about sharing such private emotions with a film crew, but Barry persuaded me that the journey should be recorded and I trusted him completely.

Cockcroft convinced the bosses at YTV to commission the programme, which was no small feat given the fact there was no guarantee there would be anything worth showing at the end of it all.

They arrived at Malaga airport with a camera crew and equipment in tow, only to fall foul of the customs and excise officers. For although they had a permit to film in Spain, the separate permit allowing them to bring their gear into the country had been left back in England. Despite pleading their case their equipment was confiscated and in desperation they contacted the local town hall, where Ashley was granted a meeting with Malaga's governor to explain their predicament.

I was talking to the governor and I just happened to say, 'Mi amigo, excellency Fraga Iribarne,' and he looked at me, picked up his phone, dialled a number and started speaking quickly in Spanish. Then he passed the phone over to me and it was Fraga Iribarne on the other end of the line. 'Ashley, how are you, what can I do for you?' So I explained our predicament and he listened patiently and then asked me to hand the phone back to the governor. So I gave him back the phone and seconds later he was signing a form allowing us to bring our equipment into the country. What a guy, we'd probably still be there now if it wasn't for him.

Having finally got their permits in order they headed inland towards the sweltering heat of Seville. They turned up at the hot and dusty gateway to the city where Ashley's grandmother had been sold to the American couple. Here Ashley met Perdita Hordern, an interpreter recommended by the British consul in

Low light before the storm, Featherbed Moss.

Seville who he had hired to help him. She had already been on the case and worked out that his grandmother's name must have been Rodriguez Rey, as it was a tradition of Spanish people to retain the maiden name of their mothers. She assumed that since the wedding certificate listed her father as Manuel Rodriguez, it meant that her mother's surname must have been Rey:

She was full of enthusiasm and explained to me that if we could trace my grandmother's birth in one of the registries it would tell me everything I needed to know, where she lived and the names of her relatives.

Finally it seemed like they were making headway, but an exhaustive tour round all of the registry offices in and around Seville proved fruitless, it appeared that the birth of Ashley's grandmother simply hadn't been recorded:

Perdita was almost as discouraged as I was and most people would have probably thrown in the towel at this point. But we sat down and went over every detail I had about my grandmother. Then she started flicking through the little red book and asked if she could borrow it for a couple of days.

This gave Ashley a bit of free time, which he used to immerse himself in painting:

I found the old quarter of Seville fascinating.

The light in the south of Spain is totally different to what you find on the Pennines so it gave me the chance to paint different variations of colour and shade.

The Rodriguez Rey family: Ashley discovers his gypsy roots.

A few days later he received a phone call from Hordern asking him to meet her in a village outside the city as she had some news. When he arrived she was waiting for him, clutching the little red book. Having spoken to local historians and genealogists the puzzle had fallen into place. As there was no record of her birth and the fact that she had been sold as a child to a dancing group pointed to only one possibility – that his grandmother was a Spanish gypsy:

I was a bit shocked, but I was also relieved that I'd finally found out the truth because this was something she'd hidden from everyone for her entire life.

Hordern had also managed to trace who she believed were his grandmother's relatives and arranged a meeting between Ashley and the head of the family, Amos Rodriguez Rey. Initially the family's patriarch dismissed the possibility that the two men could be related, but after discussing it with older family members he agreed to meet him:

The moment we met was incredible, it was like looking in a mirror, it was uncanny. We had the same face, hair, everything. We just stood there staring at each other and then he hugged me.

Ashley was then introduced to the rest of Amos's family as the story of what may have happened to his grandmother emerged. Around the time she was born one of their family members, quite possibly Ashley's great-grandmother, disappeared. The name Dolores, which she had chosen herself, was also seen as significant, as the first girl born in each branch

of the family was traditionally called Dolores. Although they had no scientific proof that they were related as DNA tests weren't available back then, the remarkable physical resemblance was evidence enough for him to be accepted as part of the family.

For Ashley, it was the start of a memorable journey that took him deep into the heart of Spanish culture. In order to prove his gypsy blood he was required to enter the bullring. A leading matador had been killed at a bullfight a few months earlier and he was understandably nervous:

There I was holding a cape with a young bullfighter and this ferocious black beast charging towards us. On the third pass one of its horns missed my groin by a whisker and I ran out of there as quickly as my legs would carry me.

Before he returned home he was invited to witness the electrifying *El Rocio*, an annual pilgrimage that dates back to the fifteenth century and involves an effigy of the Virgin Mary carried on a wagon across Andalucia. Every year in May, a seething mass of pilgrims with horses and decorated carts pour into the towns and villages of southern Spain. Many locals don traditional clothing – broad rimmed hats and country jackets for the men, and flamenco dresses for the women. Amos had brought Ashley to one of these villages in order to meet his brother Benito, a famous flamenco singer, who he hoped would confirm that he was a blood relation. For Ashley, it was an unforgettable experience:

You were literally swamped by people, the crowds and

noise were unbelievable, it was ablaze with colour like nothing I'd ever seen before. I felt the hairs on the back of my neck stand on end as I watched the young girls dancing with such skill, just like my grandmother would have done a century earlier.

After making his way through the teeming crowds he was ushered to the house of a family friend, where Benito was waiting to meet him. Before there was any time for polite introductions Benito flung his arms around him as if he was a long-lost son. There was no doubting in the eyes of the Rodriquez Rey clan that Ashley was one of their own. And the next couple of hours were spent examining the little red book, punctuated by excited chatter and umpteen glasses of vino:

They pointed out that the photographs of my grandmother dressed in her flamenco outfit and the position of her hands and feet, proved that she had been trained in Seville.

More than 12 million people tuned in to watch the subsequent YTV documentary *Once in a Lifetime – My Own Flesh and Blood* – the kind of viewing figures that producers today can only dream about. For Ashley, it had been an exhausting but unforgettable journey. A thousand miles from the rain-lashed Pennine hills, in the searing heat of Andalucia, he had found what he was looking for.

Ashley experiences the life of a bullfighter.

# 13
# The Fastest Brush in the West

Ashley's appearances on *Pebble Mill* and the success of Cockcroft's TV documentary had made him one of the most recognisable artists in the country. As his public profile grew so did the number of invitations to talk at art seminars and conferences not just in the UK but across Europe. He gave lectures on watercolour painting to fellow professional artists, as well as amateurs and art suppliers:

> You were basically explaining how the pigments worked, which paper to use and what the different brushes did. I was doing these lectures for peanuts and Anne said to me, 'Why do you keep doing this?' and I said, 'Well, you never know who might pick me up.'

And sure enough he was. He'd been doing a seminar in Milan in 1984 when he was approached by John Howe, who worked for a firm called Morrell, asking if he would be interested in doing a lecture circuit in the United States:

> He handed me his business card and said he'd be in touch. I didn't think anything of it because over the years

Ashley in America for PBS TV.

Ashley filming on location in Oregon, in the United States.

I'd been given more business cards by people than I care to remember. One thing I realized quite early on was that being an artist is a bit like being an attractive woman, everyone wants to take you to bed, but nobody wants to pay the rent.

However, a few days later he received a phone call from the same man inviting him to take part in an art exhibition in Washington DC. He agreed and turned out to be the only artist from Western Europe involved in the exhibition, held at the Washington Convention Centre. He gave a one-hour lecture before answering questions from the audience. Afterwards he was talking to a group of artists when he heard his name being mentioned over his shoulder:

I heard a voice say, 'Are these Ashley Jackson's paintings?' and I turned round and this guy was talking to one of the organizers. He walked over to me and said, 'Ashley Jackson?' And I said, 'Yes,' and he said, 'Hi there, my name's Martin Scott, I think I'm your cousin, I'm Cissie's son.' We'd never met before and then we bumped into each other completely out of the blue like that. When they say 'it's a small world', they're not kidding.

Martin was working as a researcher for NBC television, which was covering the event for one of its channels. He showed him round the famous tourist spots including the Washington Monument and Lincoln Memorial, and invited him to Baltimore to meet his family. Ashley's Washington trip was the first of several to the US capital, which in turn, led to further invitations to New York, San Francisco, Dallas and Chicago.

Sometimes as many as 3,500 people attended these international art seminars, although there were occasions when the common threads of the English language wound up getting lost in translation:

I was standing up talking to this huge audience and not knowing the subtleties of the American language I said to camera, 'I use a 4b pencil but I don't use a rubber, so if I was you I'd throw all your rubbers away because they won't help you.' When I'd said it about nine times Howard Wolf, who was one of the chief organizers, came up on to the stage and said, 'Ashley, we call them erasers,' and everyone burst out laughing because over there, of course, rubbers means condoms.

It was during one of these seminars at the Hyatt Regency hotel in Chicago that he was approached by a man called John Snyder, who asked him if he was interested in doing his own TV programme:

He came up to me afterwards and said, 'We've been watching you Ashley, and we'd like you to do a series for PBS TV.' I told him I'd like to but I only had two days left before I flew back home.

Snyder owned several art firms, including his own production company called Magic Art, and having watched Ashley at work, was convinced he was the ideal person to front a series of art shows aimed at the millions of ordinary Americans who watched Public Broadcasting Service (PBS) TV in the US:

He asked me if I had a manager and I said, 'Yes, his name's Stewart.' He wasn't really my manager he was a guy I knew in Leeds who used to be The Who's road manager. But he went along with it and he was flown over and we agreed a deal.

Ashley worked with Snyder for the next seven years, spending four weeks each year filming on location all over the US. The first series, *Ashley Jackson's World of Art*, ran from 1984 to 1988, followed by a thirteen-week series, *The Art of Ashley Jackson*, both of which were televised coast to coast on PBS TV. Because he only had a limited amount of time to spend over there during each visit, it meant he often had a hectic schedule. He had to record the half-hour outdoor programmes, as well as fourteen commercials for each series, sometimes in as little as ten days:

There were times when we used to do eight programmes in one day, although looking back I don't know how we did it. We went down the coast of Oregon and we had the editing and mixing van with us and three cameras. I'd go with the producer and we'd choose a spot, then I'd do a few sketches and the team would follow behind. We'd stand in the river mouth and work out which direction the sun was coming from and then move the easel so that we followed the sun round.

The speed at which he worked certainly impressed the film crew, who quickly dubbed him 'the fastest brush in the west':

There were no rehearsals, you were straight into it and it was hard work. But it was a challenge for me to paint different landscapes, because I didn't want people saying, 'Oh, he can only paint Yorkshire.'

Despite such a busy schedule they did have some time out which allowed Ashley to explore a side of the country that you won't find in many holiday brochures:

We were in this place called Detroit, in Oregon. We'd taken a break from filming and we went to what I call a honky tonk bar to have a drink and play some pool. It was a proper dive, there was mesh netting down in front of the stage, so if you didn't like the band that was playing you could throw your beer bottles at them, it was that kind of place. I walked up to the barmaid and asked for three margaritas. There were these two big guys sat on stools next to us and I overheard one of them say, 'I'll give you a hundred bucks to throw this Limey through the window,' and I thought it was going to kick off. The drinks arrived and this guy's pal pushed them towards us and then picked up his own tequila and said, 'This is how we do it in the States,' and downed his drink. So I said, 'In England we do it differently,' and I ordered a pitcher of margarita and said: 'We don't bother with glasses in England,' and drank it down. I ordered another three pitchers and these guys started laughing. We got talking to them and it turned out they were Presbyterian lumberjacks from the neighbouring valley and we became pals with them while we were filming there.

Wet Summers Day, Garsdale.

Towards the end of his first trip Snyder asked him if there was anything he wanted to do before he headed back home:

I told him I'd love to go and see a rodeo and he stopped me and pointed to a poster for a rodeo 400 miles away. He looked at me and grinned and said, 'leave it with me.'

In the afternoon when they had finished filming Snyder pulled up in his car with a friend and told Ashley and Stewart to jump in. They arrived a short time later at a private airfield in Salem in the hope of finding a pilot who would take them to Bend, a city on the eastern edge of the Cascade mountain range, where a rodeo was taking place that evening. Snyder was a trained pilot and normally would have flown himself, but he'd already had a couple of drinks so they found another pilot who agreed to fly them there:

We were heading right out into the wilds in this tiny, single propeller plane and Stewart said, 'You can't go on that, you'll end up like Jim Reeves.'

But after a stiff drink and a quick Hail Mary they clambered on board and were on their way:

We flew over a mountain range and when we came into land I asked where the airfield was and Snyder replied, 'You're not in England now, we're trying to find a strip to land on,' and a few minutes later we landed in a prairie field. As we climbed out the front nose sank into the ground, but we managed to lift it up and turn the plane round ready for take off later.

They made their way a few hundred yards on to a highway where they thumbed a lift in a pick-up truck:

There was a bunch of guys inside smoking some wacky backy and they asked us where we were going and it turned out they were going to the rodeo, too, so they told us to hop in. They handed us bottles of Budweiser and The Beach Boys were playing on the radio and I remember looking around and thinking, 'This is the real America and I'm getting paid to see it.'

By the time they finally arrived in Bend, the rodeo was in full swing:

I'd never seen so many cowboys, it was like something out of a Wild West film. We saw the bull riding and bronco riding and I realized why the horses and bulls jump up and down, it's because they fasten a big belt under their bellies so tight they're trying to kick it off.

Afterwards they headed to the bar for a few rounds of drinks before hitching a lift back to the plane:

We took off again and Synder turned to the pilot and said, 'Hey, why don't you let Ashley see the main strip?' So he flew down over this street and it felt we were so low you could almost touch the tops of the buildings. But as we did this we heard a series of bangs, and Snyder said, 'Jesus, they're shooting at us,' and they were. We couldn't believe it, all we could hear was the sound of gunshots pinging outside the plane.

It seems some of the cowboys and rodeo barflys had decided it would be amusing to take pot shots at this little plane which had suddenly presented itself as a target for them:

We got out of there quickly and as we were flying back over the mountains I turned to Snyder and said, 'John, that's an experience I'll never forget,' and he smiled and said, 'Glad you enjoyed it, Ashley.'

As someone who frequently flew to and from the US Ashley always travelled with British Airways and on one occasion his loyalty was rewarded:

I arrived at Heathrow and was told I'd been upgraded and one of the airline's managers escorted me to the VIP suite. I walked in and I recognized Peter Stringfellow. He had his fur coat on and I overheard him asking if he could be upgraded to first class but he was told it was full.

We got talking because we're both Yorkshire lads and a little later on as we boarded the plane he said, 'See you later, Ash,' expecting me to head into economy class, but I walked up the spiral staircase into first class and he looked at me without saying anything.

When we arrived in America we bumped into each other again at the immigration desk and he leant over and said to me, 'How much are your bloody paintings then?' He thought I always went first class, so I just shrugged my shoulders. I didn't tell him I'd been upgraded.

Sometimes, though, the joke was on him, as was the case after one particularly arduous flight to Oregon:

I was knackered as I'd just come off a fourteen-hour flight from England and Snyder was there to meet me. As I walked through customs one of the security guys said, 'Hi Ashley, I've seen you on the TV, welcome to the US of A.' This happened a couple more times with people coming up and shaking my hand and I said to Synder, 'Bloody hell the TV show must be doing well,' and he just started laughing because he'd given them all ten bucks to pretend they recognized me. But that's what he was like and we had some great times together.

Occasionally, though, Synder's charm got them in trouble:

We were in Chicago and I'd already had four meals that day with TV producers and potential clients and I was knackered so I told Snyder I was off to bed.

He hadn't been in his room long when the phone rang:

It was Laurie, Synder's PA. She said, 'I'm in the Chicago Blues Club with John and he wants you to come and join us.' So I said, 'Ok,' and she gave me the address of this club. I went out and flagged a taxi down and asked the driver to head to Lincoln Street, at which point he asked if I could be a little more specific as the street was thirty miles long. It was then that I realized just how vast America was.

By the time he got the club it was nearly two in the morning:

We were the only white people in this blues club and

Snyder was chatting up a black woman whose partner had gone to the toilet. When the guy returned Synder said to him, 'I was just keeping your seat warm.' But the woman complained that he had been coming on to her and started arguing with her boyfriend, at which point we ran out the club into a cab that Snyder had waiting outside. He always had a taxi running outside in case anything ever happened.

It was the same everywhere we went. When we were in Louisiana he told me he'd found a great jazz club but it was in an area that even the police wouldn't go into. So we went there and paid the taxis to wait. Laurie was there and so was the wife of one of Snyder's clients who was talking away in a loud voice. Then this guy came over and asked, 'Are you from South Carolina? And she said, 'Yeah,' and he started having a go at her saying, 'You had us picking cotton all our lives.' He started swearing at us and when Snyder told him to calm down you could tell what was going to happen. But Laurie always carried a gun, her husband was a police chief, and she said: 'Ashley get into the cab now, don't you worry about John he'll be right behind you.' So we ran back to the cab as fast as we could.

Despite what these escapades may suggest, they did spend most of their time either filming or checking out potential locations, and an average day usually involved working from seven in the morning until nine at night. They travelled to big cities like Boston, San Francisco and St Louis, but it was often the more remote places that proved to be the most interesting:

We went to an old native Indian reserve which took your breath away, it was this ragged wilderness right in the heart of America that probably hadn't changed much in a thousand years. We stayed in these huts, a bit like a mountain commune. There was no alcohol and all we had were a few pocket games. We were given whistles by the locals and when I asked what they were for I was told they helped ward off bears, which were in the area, because apparently they don't like the sound of whistles.

Sometimes, though, they found local communities weren't all that they seemed. During filming in the Oregon mountains they stopped at a farm, called Ma' Baker's, to ask if they could use their generator:

The farmer's wife came to the door and I noticed there were bullet holes all around the frame. I asked if we could use her electricity and she said, 'Sure'. So we thanked her and went off filming nearby. Then a little while later we were sitting having a break in this field and I started feeling a bit strange.

It was then that he realized why:

I turned to Stewart and I said, 'Hey, this is marijuana, we're lying in a field of marijuana,' and he looked around and said, 'Bloody hell you're right.'

It appeared the local farmers were growing more than just fruit and vegetables. But because it was such a remote community either the police were none the wiser, or they simply turned a blind eye:

Later that evening when we'd finished filming, this big truck appeared and a cowboy with a huge Stetson stepped out and asked if we wanted to join him and his family for a smoke, but that was a signal for us to go. They could have buried us up there and no one would ever have found us.

Like countless others before him, though, he found it an exhilarating country:

I loved America and I still do. I like the American attitude to life, they don't kick your car out of envy they say, 'I'm going to get one of those,' and wherever we went filming the police and local authorities were very accommodating because they're all so proud of their little communities.

By the time his contract finished Ashley had made forty-eight programmes over there. His repeated PBS appearances had made him as popular as the Canadian oil painting guru, Bill Alexander. Ashley said goodbye to John Snyder in Vancouver, but it was the last time he would see his friend. Snyder died a couple of years later when his plane, which he was piloting at the time, crashed in Milwaukee. However, the programmes they made together survive and are still being shown right across North America. And to this day Ashley still gets recognized in the most unlikely of places:

I was travelling up the Li River in China a few years ago doing some sketches on this boat. There were a few other tourists on board and this guy tapped me on the shoulder and said, 'It is Ashley Jackson, isn't it?' and I said, 'Yes,' and he said, 'My wife and I have watched you on TV for years.'

Heather presenting Bill Clinton with an Ashley Jackson painting.

A similar thing happened when he made an emotional return to India in 2007, for the first time in more than fifty years. He went to Rajasthan and then the city of Shimla where he briefly spent some time as a child:

I went painting all over India and in Rajasthan I bumped into a group of Americans and a couple of them came over and said they recognized me and I ended up signing a load of autographs.

Today, he continues to receive invitations to hold exhibitions in the US, where such notable figures as Bill Clinton and Rudy Giuliani have his works among their collections:

I got to talk to native American Indians and see things that most tourists don't get to experience. I look back on trips like that and think if it wasn't for my sketchbooks and paintings they would never have happened.

# 14

# Northern Tales of the Unexpected

Although Ashley has become synonymous with Holmfirth – the West Yorkshire town where he has lived and worked for more than 25 years – it is Barnsley that has shaped his life more than anywhere else:

I wasn't born in Barnsley but I see myself as a Barnsley lad, because I was bred there. Michael Parkinson once said, 'Just tell people you were conceived on the number 9 Bradford bus.' If someone asked me where I get most of my support from, I'd say the people of Barnsley, because they were always the ones who would come along to my exhibitions in London.

Although his relationship with the town hasn't always been a smooth one, as his clashes with the Barnsley Art Society prove, it toughened him up as a child:

Growing up there gave me a good foundation. In Barnsley you're told to 'shut up' twice and if you're told a third time then you'd better duck because there'll be a punch to follow.

That's the difference between Barnsley and Huddersfield. In Huddersfield they'll argue the point, in Barnsley they'll take it a step further and that's what I like about the place, not because it's violent, it isn't, but because you know where you stand with people.

But for all the rejections and criticisms he endured earlier on in his career, it's still the place where he began his artistic life. And interestingly, for a town its size, Barnsley has produced more than its fair share of famous names over the years:

It's always had to fight for attention and I think that determination rubbed off on people. If you look at some of the people who've come from Barnsley; you've got Brian Glover, Michael Parkinson, Dickie Bird, Darren Gough, Ian McMillan, Charlie Williams, Roy Mason, Arthur Scargill and Paul Sykes. All these people got to the top in their profession. But it doesn't matter if you're a 'Sir' or you're on TV, people there will still say 'Ey up, Parky,' or 'Ey up, Ashley, how's tha' doing?'

I've travelled all over the world and there aren't many places where people have the same sense of pride about where they come from, it's a bit like Sicily in that sense, which is why I call us the Barnsley mafia.

Stan Richards and Dickie Bird were among his friends from the town who Ashley used to regularly meet up with:

We'd all go for a drink on a Saturday or Sunday with our wives. We'd meet in the Railway pub in Royston and I'd walk in and Stan would be in there first and he'd say, 'It's on the counter for you lad,' and there'd be a large whisky waiting for me, and we met like this for twenty-odd years.

The actor Brian Glover, 'a lovely man and a great mate', was another of his drinking buddies. The two of them, together with Willis Hall, who co-wrote *Billy Liar* with Keith Waterhouse, Anne Pickles, a respected newspaper feature writer, and Neil Hodgkinson, former editor of the *Yorkshire Evening Post*, would meet every so often in Leeds for a long liquid lunch. Ashley remembers one in particular:

We'd been to a restaurant and gone on boozing. Brian had told us he was in a matinee at four o'clock, he was appearing in one of Chaucer's plays, *The Canterbury Tales*, at the Leeds Grand. But by the afternoon we were already a bit drunk, so we piled into a taxi and took him to the theatre. He staggered out and said, 'It's been great, I'll see you all soon.' But we told the taxi driver to wait a minute because we knew he'd be back. Sure enough ten minutes

later he came rolling out and said, 'It's fine we're not doing it this afternoon, they're going to tell everyone it's cancelled because the stage set has collapsed.' This gave him time to sober up for the evening performance.

Ashley learnt how to handle his drink earlier in his career when he went schmoozing with pressmen such as John Edwards and Malcolm Barker, respected former editors of the *Yorkshire Post* and the *Yorkshire Evening Post*:

I came up with the *Yorkshire Post* emblem which I did one drunken evening with the two of them. They taught me to drink.

He remembers meeting them both in a London pub during one of his West End exhibitions:

One of my clients from Belfast had turned up with a bottle of Bushmills, so I said to them, 'Do you mind looking after this while I go back to the gallery?' and when I came back they'd taken very good care of it, they'd supped the whole bottle.

One of the strangest tales involved Ronnie Hazlehurst, the man behind some of TV's most memorable theme tunes including *Last of the Summer Wine*, *The Two Ronnies* and *Yes, Minister*. He and Ashley had first met during the early 1980s while working on training aid films for Terry Wogan's production company and became good friends:

I was in bed one night and the phone rang, it was two in

Ashley with Bill Owen and
Brian Glover, filming the
'Loxley's Lozenge' episode
of *Last of the Summer Wine*.

The first anniversary of the opening of Ashley's Holmfirth Gallery. From left to right: Michael Cook, Stan Richards wife, Dickie Bird, Stan Richards, Gemma Craven, Fraser Hines, Mustafa Hammuri, Keith Jessop.

the morning and I reached over Anne to pick it up. It was Ronnie Hazlehurst. 'Hey Ashley,' he said, 'I've got a wonderful woman here who's fallen in love with you, I'm going to put her on to you.' I could hear a party going on in the background and then I heard this woman's voice saying, 'Hi there Ashley, it's Bertice Reading, I saw you on the TV doing your paintings, when are you coming down to London, I'd love to meet you?' So I told her that would be nice and put the phone down."

A few months later the three of them met up while Ashley was in the capital for an exhibition at the Mall Gallery:

Ronnie took us to her house in Hendon where there was a party going on. Bertice welcomed us in and Lionel Bart was there with his boyfriend. But Bertice wanted to go out for a meal with us and didn't want him tagging along and I was thinking, 'Neither do I, if he starts ordering champagne, what's the bill going to be like?' So Ronnie pretended that we were going to the BBC studios to do a recording and said we'd be back later.

Five of them, Ashley, Reading, Hazlehurst, a friend of his called Mick Rolf, a graphic artist who worked on *The Kenny Everett Show*, and a female actress who knew Reading, headed to a Chinese restaurant in North London. During the taxi ride Ashley talked to the charismatic singer:

Bertice was a wonderful woman, she was a tremendous jazz and blues singer and great fun to be with. She told me how she'd married a Swiss count when she was younger which she reckoned made her the only black princess in the world. We turned up at the restaurant where Hazlehurst in his devilment pulled the maître d' to one side and handed him a tape and asked if he would play it in the background. So we sat down for our meal and this song came on and Bertice stopped talking and said, 'Hey, that's me, they're playing my music, how about that,' and Ronnie just nodded and smiled. But that's what he was like. A few years ago he gave me his original score for *Last of the Summer Wine*. He was a big Delius fan and he wrote a little note with it saying, 'What you see, I hear in my head. Your paintings of the moors are like Delius.' I thought what a wonderful thing to say.

During the mid-1980s Ashley was in big demand both at home and abroad, but he still found time to head out onto the moors, producing around a dozen new paintings a year on top of his sketches and commissions. This might not sound prolific, but when you consider that Johannes Vermeer, a man lauded as one of the greatest painters of the seventeenth century, only produced around thirty paintings in his lifetime, it puts it in perspective. Past masters like Vermeer didn't have to contend with the same glare of publicity as artists do today, although Ashley has grown accustomed to standing in front of a TV camera over the years. Even so, there have been occasions when he's raised a few eyebrows, like the time he was being interviewed on TV by Russell Harty halfway up Pen-y-Ghent, while teaching a group of students:

As I was painting the mist was rolling in and he said to me, 'Ashley, if the Martians landed here now what do you think they would make of us standing here watching you paint?' And as he said that I said to him, 'Just look at that mist.' It was like a spirit rolling towards us and yet you could see the sky, it was like this phantom gas. And I said, 'That to me is the greatest orgasm a person can have, that's what I want to paint.' And I turned to the camera and said, 'and it lasts longer.' I never thought they would keep it in, but they did.

As well as rubbing shoulders with celebrities he has done a lot of community work away from the cameras. When the miners strike erupted in 1984 he joined pitmen on the picket line, doing sketches of the police lines. In the summer of that year, he and Roy Mason teamed up to help the striking miners. He gave Mason a number of signed limited edition prints of one of his most recognizable works, *Underbank Old Road, Holmfirth.* Mason then used his parliamentary contacts to sell them to art collectors and politicians with the proceeds going to help miners' families in Yorkshire:

I took money off them during the good times when they bought my paintings, so this was a way of supporting them when they needed help.

He also helped organize local exhibitions of kids' paintings for miners' galas:

I used to walk on the front line with people like Arthur Scargill, Michael Foot and Tony Benn, which wasn't doing me any favours in the eyes of some of those people who were buying my works. But I felt my affinity was

with the pit workers and their families.

Over the years he has helped raise millions of pounds for various charities, including Children in Need and Lineham Farm. He also spent more than three decades fundraising for the Prince's Trust. He first became involved after being introduced to Sir Angus Ogilvy, Princess Alexandra's husband. Ogilvy was both a trustee and chairman of the advisory council of the Prince's Trust, and he encouraged Ashley to get involved:

Although Sir Angus came from a privileged background he never looked down on people, he was an absolute

NUM demonstration with Jonathan Dimbleby, Bel Mooney, Arthur Scargill, Peter Purves and Ashley.

Up on Saddleworth.

I am delighted to welcome you to this special event and could not be more grateful to Ashley Jackson for so kindly agreeing to give a talk and demonstrate his remarkable skill as an artist in aid of The Prince's Trust. I have no doubt it will be a wonderful evening.

Your support tonight will directly benefit The Prince's Trust in Yorkshire and the Humber – making the most enormous difference to our work with young people in this part of the country. For those of you who are unfamiliar with what we do, The Prince's Trust exists to help young people overcome the obstacles they face and to "get their lives working" through practical support – including training, mentoring and financial assistance. My Trust focusses its efforts on those who struggled at school, have been in care, are long-term unemployed or have been in trouble with the law. Since I started The Trust thirty years ago, we have helped over half a million young people. Over the coming year, in Yorkshire and the Humber alone, my Trust aims to support 4,000 young people through a range of Trust programmes – giving them the skills and confidence to realize their potential and transform their lives.

My Trust would not be able to achieve all that it has were it not for the generosity of our supporters. Events like this one make all the difference to our ability to help the countless young people who so desperately need our support, and I owe a particular debt of gratitude to Ashley Jackson for his making this evening possible. Finally, I must express my heartfelt thanks to all of you here tonight. Your support is utterly invaluable and I do hope that you have a most enjoyable evening.

*Charles*

A letter by Prince Charles presented to guests at a charity evening where Ashley Jackson was the speaker.

gentleman and we were fighting the same cause, to help underprivileged youngsters.

During this period Ashley became a regular visitor to Kensington Palace and Highgrove. In 1986 he raised more than £60,000 for the Prince's Youth Business Trust through the sale of limited editions of his painting of *Merrick Priory Moving Light*, from his 'Vision of Turner in Yorkshire' exhibition when it opened in London. The following year he wrote to Prince Charles about the possibility of holding an exhibition to raise money for the Trust and asked if he would open it, which he agreed to. In December the Prince opened the exhibition in the unlikely surroundings of the technical room of the headquarters of Bass Yorkshire, in Huddersfield, which had been transformed into a temporary gallery:

> Prince Charles came up on the train to Huddersfield. There were crowds of people waiting to meet him and I escorted him round the gallery. He has a great interest in the arts, which sometimes gets criticized because some people think he's sticking his nose in, but I don't think they appreciate how much he cares. He has helped so many people through his Trust, which is why I call him the 'socialist Prince'.

The exhibition lasted three weeks and all twenty-five paintings on display were sold, raising a substantial amount of money for the Trust:

> I'm not one for pomp and ceremony, but to have the future King of England coming to open an exhibition for

Prince Charles opening Ashley's exhibition in Huddersfield, 1987.

me was unbelievable.

A couple of years later he had another famous visitor, but this time it was a wholly unexpected one:

Anne and I were getting ready to go out when there was a knock on the front door and when I opened it there were a couple of special branch men standing there. I could see three Jaguars parked on my driveway and one of the men said, 'Mr Jackson, we've got somebody important here who won't come inside unless he's invited.' So I walked over to one of the cars and looked

in through the window and saw it was John Major. He'd been watching a cricket match at Old Trafford and was being driven back over the Pennines when there was a problem with the communications system on board and he needed to make an urgent phone call to Downing Street. I think one of the special branch guys knew me which is why they turned up at our house.

Ashley with cricket legend Fred Trueman. Here a cricket bat is painted to raise money for charity.

Ashley with Dame Norma Major at his exhibition at the
Royal Armouries in Leeds, 2000.

Little over a year later Major became Prime Minister, following Margaret Thatcher's fall from power, and despite his hectic schedule he found time to invite Ashley and his elder daughter, Heather, for tea at 10 Downing Street:

He had just seen Jacques Delors and said he had Prince Charles coming after us. He was absolutely charming and as we were leaving he turned to Heather and said, 'If I asked your father to come down to a function, do you think he would come?'

Ashley thought he was joking but a few weeks later a card arrived through the post inviting him and Anne to Chequers, the Prime Minister's official country residence, for a party:

He invited Major, who was Foreign Secretary at the time, inside to use the phone:

He was probably on the phone for about an hour-and-a-half and after he finished he sat and had a cup of tea with us before heading off. He sent a letter of thanks and said next time we were in London to drop him a line.

As we drove in on the gravel driveway and parked up, John Major came almost running down the stone steps to greet us. He said, 'Ashley Jackson, thank you for coming,' and he greeted Anne in the same way. He was the Prime Minister, he didn't have to come out to meet us but I think it shows something of the measure of the man.

Ashley and Anne were among fifty specially invited guests,

Ashley meeting Sir John Major in Harrogate.

who included Gary Lineker and Roger Moore:

We were sat on the top table with the Prime Minister, Bryan Forbes and Nanette Newman and an old lady whose husband had first introduced him into politics.

Major was keen to show Ashley a painting on display in one of the rooms upstairs:

It was an oil painting of a lion in Africa that had been tethered to a tree. Apparently Winston Churchill hated it because he believed that a British lion should never be tethered to a tree and one day he got out his oils and painted a small mouse nibbling at the rope, so that it looked like the lion was able to break free. Later on I was telling the story to Roger Moore and I showed him the same painting, but he didn't believe me. And then Norma happened to walk past and she said, 'Yes, I've heard that story before, Ashley's quite right.'

The Majors have remained friends with Ashley and Anne over the years and Norma was among the guests who attended his 'Dawn's a New Day' exhibition at the Royal Armouries, in Leeds, in 2000:

I've met a lot of politicians in my time, but if you were to ask me who is the most sincere person in politics that I've met? I'd say John Major.

# 15

# The People's Artist

Ever since he first clashed with members of the Barnsley Art Society back in the sixties, Ashley has endured a fractious relationship with the art world in Britain. Part of this, he will admit, is down to his own deprecating attitude towards an art establishment, which he believes is riddled with 'snobbery and pseudo-intellectuals'. However, he also realized early on in his career that his chances of becoming a successful artist would be greatly enhanced if he could get his paintings exhibited in London's prestigious galleries. He has enjoyed some notable success over the years – he's had works accepted by the Royal Society of British Artists, the Royal Watercolour Society (RWS) and enjoyed a string of one-man exhibitions at the Royal Institute of Painters in Water Colours (RI):

It's nice to get your works hung in these places but I'm not a society man, it's a bit like Lowry said, 'If you can't make the grade on your own, then join an establishment.'

But he's also had to contend with his fair share of rejection:

I've had my work accepted by the Royal Academy but

not hung there, they said it had been 'crowded out'. But it's difficult for northern artists unless you have an agent, and I've never had one, because it takes time and money to keep going down to London and if you're not working you're not making a living.

He didn't take kindly when he was told by an RI member that he had been 'a whisker away' from being invited to join:

I told him where he could stick it. I don't need letters after my name to show people that I'm any good, the only thing that matters is can I do the job. And as long as the public are buying my works then I'm happy to let them be the judges.

He has long been an advocate of taking 'art to the people', a mantra he's repeated many times over the years. So much so that it's led to him being called the 'people's artist', although it's not a title he's awarded himself as some people may think:

I didn't call myself that, the first person who used the

phrase was Arthur Scargill. We were at a miners' rally in Doncaster and he was presenting Tony Benn with one of my paintings and he described me as 'the people's artist' because I was a working-class lad.

It's an interesting point, because although he was surrounded during the early part of his childhood by what he calls 'the gin and tonic set' in the Far East, that life ended when he arrived in England. The posh boy who spoke the Queen's English was slowly replaced by a working-class lad whose vowel sounds were as flat as the caps of the Pennine peaks he went on to paint. But if his personality has altered over time, his views on art have remained resolutely egalitarian:

I haven't changed my attitude to the arts, I believe it's about making art accessible to the ordinary working classes. I've been told many times that I've jeopardized my career by criticizing the art establishment, but if I don't agree with something then I'll say so.

He believes that ordinary men and women have been disenfranchised from art:

If you go down the street whether it's Holmfirth, Leeds, or London, and ask people who Antony Gormley is, there's a fair chance you'll get a few blank looks, and that's because art has never been properly taught to the masses. But artists like Gormley are trying to bring art back to the people, to get them talking about it. People either like the Angel of the North or they don't, but they look at it and they talk about it and that's what's important.

He believes that our municipal galleries, which should be inspiring and educating people, are under too much pressure:

I was told privately at one gallery that they clicked 500 people through the doors before they opened, because if they didn't they were worried the council would close them down.

Others, he claims, spend too much time trying to get people through their doors, rather than concentrating on good art:

At Leeds Art Gallery they had what's called a sound sculpture, so you could hear the sound of water inside and outside. They have so much space in the gallery and yet they have things like this. I said to one of the staff, 'I'm not a philistine but can you tell me, do you get a lot of people coming in to listen to this? And he said, 'Yes, because you can hear it outside in the street, but some of them do come in asking if this is the baths.'
    It's right that we have new ideas in art otherwise nothing would ever change, but let's explore it with skill rather than some sod sat somewhere thinking, 'How can I get some money out of the Arts Council?'

In the past he has found private galleries intimidating, so he says it's little wonder that members of the public feel the same way:

You go into some galleries and you feel like you've got

Brown Light on Langsett Moor.

to walk around on tip-toes, because you'll get a dirty look if you make a slight noise, but they're not libraries. We should be encouraging families to go to galleries, but we don't, if you go into a gallery people say, 'Shhh.' They're more like morgues and the attitude seems to be 'don't laugh in here this is serious stuff' and that makes me sad.

Tom Stoppard once remarked that 'imagination without skill gives us modern art'. It's a sentiment that Ashley agrees with:

The problem I have with a lot of modern art is it's missing the skill. When you look at a work whether it's a watercolour, or a piece of abstract art, you want to go, 'Wow, how have they done that?' But it seems a lot of artists are more bothered about shocking people so they can make headlines.

At the end of the day a pile of bricks is a pile of bricks. It's not art. It can have a fancy title and people can say it represents modern life crumbling, or whatever they like. But those bricks will be transported to galleries by a team of workers, not by the artist himself, where's the skill in that?

The Turner Prize was set up in 1984 to celebrate contemporary art in Britain, but many people, including Ashley, believe it has become more about causing controversy than celebrating brilliance. Former winners include avant-garde artist Chris Ofili, known for his vibrant paintings bedecked with elephant dung, and minimalist artist Martin Creed, whose prize-winning work entitled *The Lights Going On and Off*, did exactly what it said on the tin. But Ashley believes this only alienates ordinary people from art:

If you're a real artist, whether you're a sculptor, a painter, or into conceptual art, you have to put your soul into it, otherwise what's the point? It's one thing to draw something, to do a scribble and pass it on to a team of technicians, but where's the skill in that? I like to think I'm one of the band of artists that doesn't have to put 'this way up' on the back of their work.

So what about artists like Damien Hirst and Tracey Emin, who have undeniably helped make people more aware about modern art, even if they don't like it?

I don't talk badly about fellow artists, because if you're doing well you should be too busy concentrating on what you're doing to be bad-mouthing other people. It's those who aren't busy who usually have a go at others. So good luck to Damien because he has got people through the doors and into galleries. There were a lot of eyebrows raised when his famous *Shark in Formaldehyde* sold for six-and-a-half million quid. Now Lowry would've have said, 'I don't want to have a look at the cheque, show me the bank statement.' But I think there are people who have so much invested in some artists that they can't afford to see them fail.

He feels the word 'contemporary' has been hijacked by the so-called experts and academics:

Ashley with sculptor Graham Ibbeson at their Knightsbridge Exhibition, 2007.

They use it when they're talking about a pile of dung – is it abstract, is it Pointillism? No it's a pile of dung. But they call it contemporary because they don't know what else to call it. So what about artists like myself and Graham Ibbeson and Antony Gormley? We're contemporary and we're skilled, but the word 'contemporary' is now being used to give a name to all the unskilled stuff that passes for art.

Despite his dislike of much of what passes for contemporary art, he does admire many modern artists including Picasso, Miro and Hockney, as well as sculptors like Jacob Epstein, Henry Moore and Ibbeson – 'craftsmen' he calls them:

You've got Picasso at the top of the tree and then there's everybody else. There have been some great experimental artists but he was the best. You look at his portraits and you can see a hundred different perspectives in one go, but you have to study art to be able to do that. It's the same with Hockney, he's a great draughtsman and you can see that in his works.

At the same time, however, he rails against what he perceives to be the inherent snobbery of Britain's art establishment:

If people don't think there's snobbery in the art world then they should ask themselves would Rolf Harris get into Saatchi's gallery? And if not, why not, because he's certainly got the skill. He's done more for art on TV than probably anyone else ever has and compared to some of the artists who've won the Turner Prize he's a genius, but the art world turns its nose up at him.

He has little time, either, for art critics:

I make a living out of art but a lot of the so-called critics and experts don't paint or draw, they're not artists yet they call themselves experts. Some of the lads I taught in prison have more talent than some of those who call themselves professionals today. If you look at some of the African artists who create those beautiful, tall sculptures, they haven't been to art school. But Alberto Giacometti got some of his ideas for his stretched men and women from this kind of art.

When it comes to his own influences there are two men who stand head and shoulders above the rest. While Lowry was the mentor he had the good fortune to know, Turner was the great light painter who inspired him to pick up a brush:

When I came to England I discovered Turner as a young lad. I was probably about thirteen when I fell in love with his work and then Thomas Girtin's.

He believes the period from 1750 through to 1850 was the greatest in England's art history:

Turner was a visionary and, for me, he's the greatest painter Britain's ever produced. He was before his time, he was doing impressionism before French artists like Monet and Renoir came along.

In his landscape paintings he frequently merged separate drawings from his sketchbook into the finished painting:

Turner travelled across the north of England and he went to places like Gordale Scar, but rather than just painting what he saw he exaggerated the size, and because there was obviously no cameras and TV in those days nobody knew any better.

He says Turner is in a 'different league' to him:

Turner was a romantic painter, I'm a melancholy one.

Certainly there are stark differences between the two men's paintings. While Turner's burnished skies have an empyrean glow, Ashley's possess a more brooding, Stygian quality. Although it's interesting that both men have been criticized for being too commercial:

He suffered the same thing from the art establishment in the eighteenth century. He was a hustler who knew how to promote himself and he made a lot of money, which some people didn't like.

They may not have liked it, but it didn't stop some of them trying to cash in when the opportunity arose:

John Ruskin befriended him at the end of his life and Turner told him one day, 'My doctor says that I'm dying and I could even go tomorrow, so if you want some of my works you can have them half price.' Ruskin went

Rain and Wind.

away to think about it and came back later on only to find Turner up and about and painting away. Ruskin asked if the deal was still on and Turner shook his head and said, 'No, I just wanted to see what you would do.'

The question of conflict between creativity and commercialism in his work is one Ashley has repeatedly been asked. It has led to him being labelled with such unwanted sobriquets as 'the patron saint of telegraph poles', which has followed him around for more than thirty years:

There's always someone who wants to knock what you're doing and take a pop at you. If I could afford it I wouldn't sell any of my paintings because each one is the result of a lot of toil and sweat. But I'm a realist and at the end of the day if I don't sell my work then I'll lose my living, so I've got to keep working to survive.

Everyone thinks, 'Ashley Jackson, he's got this, he's got that,' but it's taken a hell of a lot of time and effort to get where I am now. Anne and I didn't have a holiday for nearly twenty years and we haven't got a villa in Spain stashed away. Every time I did exhibitions abroad I financed them, even though I was invited, because that's how it works. I had to pay to get my paintings across to these places, it wasn't done for me.

So those who accuse him of having turned making money into an art form are missing the point:

When I started out all I wanted to do was be an artist but you've got to be a publicist as well as. It's alright someone saying they're the greatest artist in the world, but what use is it if people don't know who you are, so you've got to market yourself. It's about survival, you can't just sit on your laurels and expect the public to come to you.

At the same time, he says, artists have to earn the right to charge large sums of money for their work:

That's one of the problems with some young artists today, they think people should be paying big money for their paintings straight away, which is barmy, because if I was starting off today my paintings would be around £150.

In one sense it's easier for artists today because there's this cushion called grants, but at the same time it's hard because it's become more competitive. I've never asked for a grant and I've never been approached for one. For me, it's a bit like your dad giving you money. I think if something's worth it you have to fight for it. Barnsley taught me that, it taught me to have that fire in my belly. No one owes you a living, you don't go cap in hand, you find your own way.

Another tag he's frequently labelled with is that of the dreaded 'professional Yorkshireman', which perhaps isn't helped by the fact that over the course of his career he's styled himself as 'the Yorkshire artist':

A reporter recently asked me if I thought of myself as a professional Yorkshireman and I said, 'No I'm proud of my county, but I don't shove it down people's throats.'

Nevertheless, he's fiercely protective of his relationship with the Yorkshire landscape:

Another watercolour artist called John Blockley came up to look at my works one day and he said sniffily, 'Oh, I see you paint in the same vein as I do.' And I thought, 'That's crap, I don't read your books, I'm not trying to copy what you're doing. Yorkshire's made me the artist, not you.'

Although he revels in his role as an art outsider, he concedes it may have hampered his career. He was once asked at a dinner party by a well-to-do guest what was on his CV to which he replied: 'Working-class, done well', something he wears like a badge of honour:

Anne has said to me before, 'You could have gone a lot further in the art world, but the reason you haven't is because you're not a diplomat and diplomats are paid to lie.'

As someone approaching the twilight of his career, he sees it as his responsibility to help other, younger artists:

If a young professional artist comes to see me, and they do from time to time, I tell them everything. I don't hold anything back because I remember Ron Darwent once saying to me, 'I'm going to teach you everything there is to know in this craft, because the tutor that holds back from his student only does so because they're not truly competent – and I'm good, lad.' And that's my feeling, because there are too many old bulls out there who won't pass the baton on to the next generation. You get other artists who moan about the fact that they can't afford to buy their own paintings. I can't afford some of mine once they're up for sale. But it's up to the artist if they want to keep their work or not, so of course they can afford it.

When he first set out to become an artist a lot of people scoffed and said he'd never make it. But the array of paintings that adorn the walls of his Holmfirth gallery are testament to the fact that he has. His original watercolours, which range in price from £600 to £35,000, are instantly recognizable as one man's work – the signature angry skies, the looming, blustery landscapes and ethereal light. He also sells limited edition prints, pencil sketches, Christmas cards and even specially designed china cups. But if his works have almost become a brand in their own right, they still retain a broad appeal:

We get all sorts of people coming through our doors and we make sure there's something that everyone can afford. For fifteen pounds you can get a framed and mounted Ashley Jackson print and I still sign them all on the back, because art should be affordable to everyone. The greatest accolade I can get is when people bump into me and say, 'Do you know my wife and I were going over the moors and I said to her, 'Look it's an Ashley Jackson sky.' I still find that incredible.

Flight Hill Above Holmfirth.

# 16

# The King of Prussian Blue

Ashley with Liz Dawn of *Coronation Street* fame on *A Brush with Ashley* for YTV.

By the early 90s, Ashley's TV contract in the US had finished and he was spending more time painting on the moors and organizing exhibitions in the UK. But he still had his old contacts at YTV and given the success of his programmes in America it wasn't long before the call came to see if he would be interested in doing something similar over here:

I'd known Graham Ironside for many years and he asked me if I would come and do a pilot. I was asked if I had my own production company and I'd been advised to say, 'Yes,' even though I didn't have one. So when I was asked what it was called I said H and C, which I named after my daughters Heather and Claudia.

The pilot programme was recorded and *A Brush With Ashley* was born. The first series consisted of six, half-hour programmes which were screened during afternoons. Initially it involved three art students, chosen by Ashley from around Holmfirth, who joined him to paint on location all over Yorkshire, in places likes Haworth, Staithes and Robin Hood's Bay. Despite its slot on daytime TV the first series pulled in over a third of the

Filming *A Brush with Ashley* for YTV.

The loan paid for the cameras, crew, editing equipment and everything else that goes into making a TV programme:

I'm the risk taker and I was gambling with our future.

It meant a fraught summer while they filmed the series and awaited the outcome of the franchise battle. They finally found out in November when Ashley rang the chief executive's office:

I spoke to his secretary who said she'd call back because they were waiting for a fax coming through. She rang five minutes later and said they'd got the franchise.

Filming on location in Yorkshire.

viewing audience – a remarkable figure for any programme, but especially one about art. In 1992, Clive Leach, who was then boss of YTV, approached him about doing another series. However, the offer came with a caveat. Because YTV was in the middle of a bid with a rival consortium for the ITV franchise in Yorkshire, he couldn't guarantee that the series would happen. This meant Ashley would have to stump up the cash himself. He was given a letter of intent by YTV to buy the series on the proviso their bid won the franchise. If it didn't he could then sell it to another company, as long as they were interested:

I discussed it with Anne and we decided to go to the bank and take out a loan to finance the six programmes. We basically risked the house on someone's word.

The gamble had paid off and he headed down to the YTV studios in Leeds to celebrate:

I became the blue-eyed boy over there with the bosses because I'd risked everything.

*A Brush With Ashley* went on air the following year and it was the last time the artist had to risk the family home to finance a project.

The series ran for a total of nine series up until 2001, and compared to the tight filming schedules he was used to in the US, he found it relatively easy:

In America sometimes we were doing as many as eight programmes a day. But in England it would take all day to do just one.

Although he had painted live on air while working at Pebble Mill, he says it was his time spent in America that really taught him how to paint for the cameras:

I would see where the sun was and just follow it round. When the light was dropping the cameraman would signal to me how much time I had left, and I learnt how to talk to the cameraman while I was painting.

It was a style he adopted when filming in Yorkshire:

I wasn't given a script because the director said if they did that it would come out in pidgin English, so I just explained what I was doing and that seemed to make it flow better.

Ashley with Fred Trueman at Kilnsey Crag for *A Brush with Ashley.*

Despite his apparent ease painting in front of a camera crew, he admits he found it difficult to begin with:

When I was a kid my stepfather told me that I was thick and this had kicked my self-confidence, so to go on television took a lot of hard work and to this day I still get nervous.

It was Sid Waddell who gave him a tip on how to handle interviews and TV appearances:

He said to me one time, 'When you're being interviewed on TV and you're asked a question, don't lean forward to

answer it because people watching will think you're making an excuse for something.' He said what you should do is hang your arm over the chair casually and that stops you moving forward and makes you appear relaxed, even if you're a bag of nerves like I was.

But David Holdgate, former managing director of programmes at YTV, believes Ashley has helped bring art to the people:

He's made it accessible. Something like the *South Bank Show* has done a lot of good work promoting artists but it's seen as a high brow programme. The beauty of Ashley's TV series is it brought home to people how real art is in their lives.

There have been a variety of art-based programmes made in Yorkshire over the years but nobody has achieved what Ashley has. There was never any snobbery with him, he just has that rare ability to demonstrate the value of art to ordinary people through his passion and enthusiasm.

His TV series became a staple of afternoon viewing during the nineties, although it wasn't just students and housewives who watched his show, as Ashley discovered one day when he was driving home with his daughter Heather:

We were on this country road and a lorry was coming from the opposite direction. The road was too narrow for

Ashley painting with students on one of his Paint Days for YTV.

us to both pass so he signalled at me to come forward and as I did he pointed to the window, so I stopped and wound it down and he did the same. And he said in this thick Yorkshire accent, 'It's thee, fucking good programme.' He had tattoos all up his arms and I had my daughter sitting next to me and then he shouted, 'Show us your ring,' so I held up my hand and he said, 'It is, it's fucking thee, prussian blue kid, prussian blue.' I used to always reel off the colours I was using, prussian blue, burnt sienna, red and yellow. And he said, 'Tha's for workers, kid, tha's our artist,' and off he went. I thought to myself, 'Well, I must be doing something right'.

By the third series the producers decided to change the format. So instead of teaching students how to paint watercolours, he was joined by celebrities including Fred Trueman, Brian Glover, Liz Dawn, Dickie Bird and Kathy Staff:

They stood out in the pouring rain at times, but they were great fun to work with. Kathy Staff told me that the weekend before she came on my programme she got a call from the *Daily Mail*, asking if she would do a photo shoot for them in Paris. She thought it was a bit strange but she asked if her husband could come along and they had said yes. So she packed her bags ready for this trip but when the photographer turned up at her house it turned out they wanted to do a photo shoot in Paris, Holmfirth, for an article about *Last of the Summer Wine*, so she went along with it because she didn't want them thinking that she thought they were whisking her off to France.

The popularity of his TV programme led to a flurry of offers from publishers keen to cash in on his popularity. 1992 saw the release of *Painting in the Open Air*, which was followed by a raft other titles, including *A Brush with Ashley* and *Ashley Jackson's Yorkshire Moors – a love affair*. He also began doing an art workshop called, *An Evening With Ashley Jackson*, touring libraries and theatres across the north of England:

We packed out a lot of the venues. We turned up at one place and there were people queuing outside trying to get in, I couldn't believe it.

Richard Whiteley shares a joke with Ashley.

The mid-90s brought a string of notable exhibitions. In the spring of 1995 he embarked on a touring exhibition called *Here's to You Dad*, not only to commemorate the life of his father, but as a mark of respect to all those who lost their lives in the Far East during the Second World War. This was followed two years later by a major one-man retrospective exhibition called *Earth, Wind and Fire* at the Lowry Gallery in Salford. It featured Ashley's haunting impressions of many well-known landscapes captured during a tour of the British Isles. It was particularly poignant for him to be invited to hold an exhibition in the gallery of his old friend and mentor.

To some, Ashley was now as much a TV celebrity as he was an artist, and in 1996 he was voted 'Yorkshire Arts and Entertainment Personality of the Year'. He had also become a regular fixture on the cruise ship lecture circuit, travelling on some of the most prestigious liners in the world including the SS Canberra and the QE2, and working alongside well-known figures such as Sir Peter Blake, Jim Bowen and Hugh Scully. Throughout this time he continued doing his TV series, but after more than fifty episodes he decided he'd taken the programme as far as he could:

I still get people asking me why I'm not on the telly any more. But the reason is, I backed off. I know some people might disagree but I don't want to be a TV personality, I want to be remembered for my paintings.

He began spending more time ensconced in his studio at home and it was here that he was working on the afternoon of September 11, 2001:

I had my sketchbooks out and I was painting away, I was listening to Steve Wright's radio show when he said that a plane had just crashed into one of the Twin Towers. Like many people I presumed it was just an accident, but then Claudia rang me up and said, 'Dad, switch your telly on.' So I downed tools and Anne and I sat glued to our TV like millions of other people as those terrible events unfolded.

Several hours later, as the world struggled to comprehend the enormity of what had happened, he went back into his studio:

I tore up the painting I'd been working on and I got out some sketches I did of the Hudson while I was on board the QE2.

Just two weeks earlier Ashley had been to the top of the World Trade Centre building during a visit to New York:

I felt compelled to do something and I worked from seven o'clock that night, right the way through to seven the following morning.

He worked on the painting every day for the next three weeks until it was finished, before sending it to Newcastle to be framed:

A few weeks later the phone rang when I happened to be in. It was George Robertson, Secretary-General of Nato. He said, 'I understand you've done a painting of the Twin Towers that we would like at Nato. How much do

Ashley with George Robertson and R Nicholas Burns, the US permanent representative to NATO.

there thought my painting was more powerful than all the photographs of the towers being blown up, because it made the hairs on the back of their necks stand on edge and that makes me feel proud.

Today, his painting, *The Day The World Changed*, can still be seen at NATO's headquarters, a vivid reminder of an event it seems impossible to forget.

Lord Robertson unveils Ashley's work at NATO Headquarters.

you want for it?' I told him I didn't want any money, so I gave it to them.

One of Lord Robertson's staff had driven passed the gallery and spotted the painting in the window. It was sent to Brussels and Lord Robertson invited Ashley and Anne to stay with him at his NATO residence for a special unveiling ceremony:

We were having dinner and he turned to me and said, 'By the way, tomorrow you do know you're giving a speech and you'll be talking to nineteen ambassadors of the world?' He also told me that everyone who worked

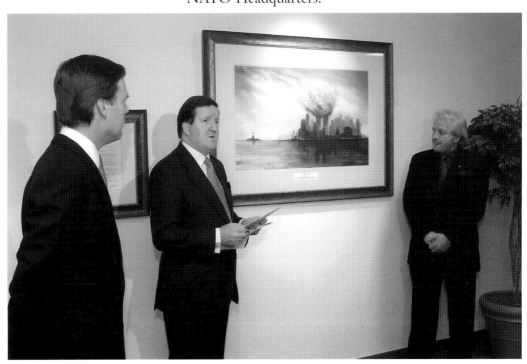

*The artist with some of the celebrity guests who appeared on 'A Brush with Ashley'.*

Ashley with Helen Sharman,
the first woman in space.

Ashley with Liz Dawn.

Ashley with John Baxter.

Rain and Wind over Dingley Moor.

# 17

# A Love Affair with Nature

When Ashley first clapped eyes on the Pennine hills as a youngster he was captivated by what he calls these 'frozen seas', which contrasted sharply with the flat, humid conditions he had grown accustomed to in India and Malaya. Yet it was in the Far East where he first came across watercolour painters:

When I was a young lad I used to knock around with the Indian and Chinese boys. Some of their parents would paint outside their homes and it was fascinating watching them do these watercolours. They did them flat or at a 45-degree angle and I wanted to be able to do that. Oils didn't interest me, even though the climate out there is better-suited to oil painting because in the humidity oils last much better than watercolours.

Those who've studied Ashley painting have often commented on how quickly he works, something he believes can be traced back to his days in Malaya:

I spent a lot of time watching the peasant shopkeepers who seemed to spend most of their spare time painting.

They were incredibly dextrous and I realized even back then that the faster you get an original idea down on paper the purer it is.

While at art school he spent every spare moment working on his technique:

Every so often I would give myself a good kick up the backside because they weren't progressing. But one important lesson I learned from Stanley Chapman was to take six steps with your back to the painting and look at it through a mirror, because this way it gives you a fresh eye and you can see your faults.

Stanley Chapman co-founded the now defunct Yorkshire Watercolour Society with Ashley. And it was Chapman who introduced him to Joe Pighills, 'a brilliant half-deaf Dales artist', Percy Monkman, 'a lovely Capo di Monte type fella from Bradford' and Tom Sykes, from Otley:

I would go out painting with all these old codgers and

they took me under their wing, because I was a young artist starting out. They were very well placed amateurs in watercolour painting. We all used to swap works and I've got a couple of Joe's paintings including one where just as he was signing his name he sneezed and splattered the painting, I've still got that hanging on my wall at home with his DNA on the paper.

Ashley paints in the tradition of the English School of watercolours which doesn't use white or black paint, so the only white that's visible is the paper itself:

I used to outline my works with felt pen and I did that for a reason. Because right from the beginning I was told that watercolours were wishy-washy, and when they were hung next to an oil painting they often looked insipid. So I wanted to get some power into my works and for the first ten years I did felt work and painted over the top.

In the early days it was a battle to get his paintings noticed:

I had to try and convince the hardnosed art world of London to display my works, which was like banging your head against a brick wall unless you happened to be a celebrity artist. They would tell me that to put one of my paintings up they would have to take two others down and I turned round and said, 'You can't paint Yorkshire with a ruler,' which obviously didn't go down very well.

Gradually, over the years, he reached the point where he stopped using felt pens and allowed his watercolours to stand on their own merits:

A lot of artists create a bohemian image for themselves, but I've never been interested in that. It's always been about my work, which is all done freehand.

There are no gimmicks in my paintings now. Some artists use masking fluid, but if you do that you've got to stick to that because you've decided where the light is, but the light can move during the day. So I don't know where the white areas will be until I start painting and I can see where the light is coming from.

Another trick that's sometimes used when you want a bit of white on your watercolour, is you paint it yellow with masking fluid and once you've painted all over it and done your washes, you pull it off with a putty rubber and it leaves a white space. But I don't do any of that because it leaves a hard line, I do it naturally.

A traditional English watercolour painting only requires a minimum of six washes, one layered on top of the other, but sometimes Ashley will have as many as thirty:

I can only do that because I know which colours will go opaque and those that are transparent, and when somebody asks how do I know I tell them it's about skill and apprenticeship. If someone doesn't know the alphabet then they can't write, and it's the same with painting.

Nature's Art, Greenfield Moor.

An exhibition at the House of Commons for the Yorkshire Watercolour Society, of which Ashley was the chairman for ten years.

His own artistic apprenticeship has taken him to some of the most famous art galleries in the world:

I've been to the Guggenheim and Metropolitan museums in New York and the Prada in Madrid. I've stood and gawped at Velazquez's work because even though they're portraits they have the power of light, which you need. And that's all I do with my paintings, I search for light.

It is this ability to capture light on paper that powers his work and which compels him to return time and again to the Pennine hills of Yorkshire:

I only go out painting between September and March because that's when you have moving clouds. During the summer you have a kind of saucepan lid and there's not much in the way of cloud shapes. But I get people joking, 'I thought you'd be up on the moors with it being miserable?' But that's graveyard dank and the light comes round the cloud, rather than through it.

There was a time when he would go out no matter how bad the weather was:

When I was younger I would take everything with me and sit out in all kinds of conditions and paint and it was a nightmare trying to keep the paper dry and not damage it. My doctor eventually told me not to paint outside in February because every year around that time I'd have to take a week off work because I was breathing in the algae and coming down with chronic chest infections.

Nowadays he usually takes the sketches back to his studio at home where he transforms them into the watercolours that have become his calling card:

I've got a great blues collection, Lightnin' Hopkins, Sonny Terry and Brownie McGhee, which I play while I'm working and later on I might have a glass of whisky. Now working conditions can't get much better than that for me.

Although he may only go up on the moors three or four times a month these days, he still follows the same routine armed with a rucksack containing a sketchpad, some watercolours and a few brushes and pencils:

I take two or three sheets of paper clipped to my board so the paper is kept clean, but I don't take an easel because that's extra weight to carry, I only use an easel for demonstrations. I just go off walking and I might come away only having done a couple of sketches. When I go out painting I need that 'wow' factor. If the hairs stand up on the back of my neck, like when you hear a great piece of music, then I'll do a small sketch, or a couple of lightning sketches, so I can capture the movement of the light and the wind.

It's an intense, but euphoric, process:

Picasso used to say he had to have an affair with his

models before he could paint them nude, so I don't paint nudes, I paint landscapes.

I paint the moors because I've always had this eerie, almost forbidding feeling, that there is something powerful and mysterious at work and I feel the spirit of the place. When I go out and paint I have my flask of whisky with me and I have the odd swig and think about all the people who've passed through this way over the centuries.

I get a feeling when I'm up there that's a bit like the first time I held hands with a girl, or the first time I had sex. Some people take drugs for escapism, but painting is my escapism.

It's something he never grows tired of:

I love going up on to the Moors and the Pennines because it reminds me how fortunate I am to be able to make a living out of painting mother nature. I never stop getting excited by it.

However, being imbued with the spirit of the place is one thing, having the ability to use that to create paintings capable of taking your breath away, is another:

The light comes to you, rather than the other way round. You're constantly trying to capture the moment. You can talk to people about the technical skill involved, but you can't explain how you created a certain painting because at the time you're immersed in it, you don't have time to analyze it.

Having spent so much time studying the landscape he has learnt how to read its ever-changing moods:

Up on the Pennine hills the sky is as important as the landscape. It's the reflection of the sky that creates this spirit and when you're up there on your own you can sense the power of mother nature. I've been painting in the middle of nowhere five miles from the nearest road and I'll suddenly hear voices telling me to get off the moor and sure enough half an hour later the storm clouds descend. The hill farmers who work the land will tell you what it's like and there's more bad weather than Torremolinos weather.

It is this unpredictability that has helped forge the character of the landscape:

The moors are masculine. You can picnic on them and later the same day you could die on them, the clouds roll in and the whole atmosphere changes. I sometimes get asked why I don't paint Cornwall, but to me that's manicured, whereas the moors and Pennine hills are wild. But this frightens some people and they daren't go up there on their own because they don't like the idea of untamed nature.

When it comes to the Pennine moors everyone has their favourite spot. For some it's the exposed plateau above Calderdale, for others it's the unforgiving lunar landscape of Saddleworth Moor, or the lush upper valleys of the River Nidd. For Ashley it's all what he calls his 'mistress':

Autumn Solitude.

I never get bored by the landscapes because it's a big old area and the greatest challenge in painting the Yorkshire Pennines is the flat, table-tops. It's not like the Lake District, or the Scottish Highlands, where they have peaks so as the pyramid goes back into the distance it gets smaller. Painting a flat piece of land two thousand feet above sea level and giving the impression that you're not in Lincolnshire, without any vertical objects taking you into it, like trees or telegraph poles, that's difficult, because they give you perspective. It's much harder to paint, and paint well, when you're only being taken in by the light.

So it's easy to paint Robin Hood's Bay, or Flamborough Head, because you have a ready-made composition through the buildings. But the hardest thing to do is paint an empty space and give it life and mystery – it's easy to paint something, but it's difficult to paint nothing.

Ashley has painted all over the world and he uses these trips to help him when he goes back out on the moors:

People have asked me why I wanted to go to America and see the skies there and the answer is it gives me more inspiration when I come back to Yorkshire's Pennines, because it refreshes your mind's eye.

I don't mind if a critic comes along and doesn't like my work because I'm painting for myself, not for them. I've heard people say, 'Oh, well he just paints the Yorkshire Moors and the northern uplands,' but so what? Lowry did the industrial landscapes, Monet did his lilies and

Rubens was famous for his big women, but no one criticizes them.

He is more passionate about his paintings than many people realize:

I get quite emotional about my works because I don't churn them out. I couldn't tell you how long some of them take because I don't time myself. It might sound silly to some people but these are my children and if someone walked in to my gallery and said they wanted a painting to go with their colour scheme I wouldn't sell it to them. I've refused to sell to people three or four times, they can get an interior designer if they want to do that.

In his younger days Ashley was more discriminate about which paintings he kept and which ended up in the bin:

For every painting up on my gallery wall, maybe three or four were torn up. But it was Lowry who told me not to tear them up, 'Don't be the judge of your own paintings,' he would say to me. So what I do now if it's not working is I turn the paper over and start again. If I'm out on the moors and I see a lovely indigo sky with the light breaking through and hitting the moorland like a torchlight, then I'll think, 'Wow, I'm going to get that sky.' You then mix your colours but if you're one or two shades out when you hit the paper, it's no use then going and painting an abstract orange sky, you may as well sit in your studio at home and do that. But it takes experience and confidence to know when you've got it right.

The artist at work on the Yorkshire Moors.

Top Withens.

However, he remains his own harshest critic:

When I look back over the last fifty years, I can see the difference in my works and sometimes I feel like buying up all the ones I did years ago when I started out and tearing them up. As a professional artist you can fall into the trap of doing the same layout. You can tell when you look at your own paintings, or other people's works, that if they're being lazy they'll have a road or a path leading in to the picture, or a row of trees. If you don't have roads leading in it makes you work harder and if you're working harder you're paintings will be better.

What separates amateurs from professionals, he says, is one does pictures, the other creates paintings:

To be able to draw and paint you need to know about composition, you need to know about perspective and a tutor can teach you that. But although you may be able to paint it doesn't mean you're a painter.

We all learn how to write, but not many of us are authors. It's that little segment inside you that makes you want to do it and it's the artist's soul that makes the difference between a picture and a painting.

You see people's character through their art, just like you do in music. If you hear a piece of music by Strauss or Beethoven, you know it's them, and it's the same with modern musicians like Sting or Mark Knopfler, you recognize their voice and their style.

Interestingly, and perhaps contrary to what some people might think, Ashley's work has evolved over the years:

I feel that I'm forever experimenting and going deeper into my work. A lot of my paintings now are almost abstract, but you can still read them and that's important because if you're writing a love letter you want the other person to be able to read it.

This is borne out by his output over the last decade or so, which includes much of his best work. In one of his snowstorm scenes of Saddleworth Moor he creates what he calls 'echoes of light' to create a snapshot of winter at the edge of hell. In *Greenfield Moor* and *When God moves – storm over Deer Hill*, there is a similar sense of staring into a primeval world as the forces of light and shadow rage against one another:

When I'm up in the moors I'm there on my own which people think must be lonely, but although I can be a sociable character I enjoy the solitude that painting gives me. The Duchess of St Albans said to me once, 'Ashley, you're melancholy.' And that's true, part of me is.

As well as adding new, bolder dimensions to his work, he is also creating bigger canvasses. His 50 inch by 40 inch, double-elephant sized, paintings outstrip anything produced by watercolourists like Turner and Gainsborough. Proof that age hasn't just brought experience, but self-assurance too:

When I paint I still have in mind my automatic checks; perspective, composition, and so on. But I remember my old art teacher Miss Hayden telling me when I was a teenager, 'As you get older you'll have more patience,' and it's true, I'm not a young man in a hurry any more.

Despite this he remains an instinctive, rather than academic artist:

I would like to be known as the guy who painted the love letters of the moors which he took from mother nature. The Chinese say that the first fifty years are the hardest in painting and I've just done fifty years. But I'm still learning even now and I still haven't done my best painting.

# 18

# The Van Gogh of Kirklees

Dr Richard Seddon, former director of Sheffield City Art Galleries, once said this of Ashley's art:

> The skies – thinly washed in, weep their pale greys and blues down the picture on to black trees that press against the sky like a child's fingers on a wet and dirty window pane. Indeed in all the pictures, it is raining, or it is going to rain, or has just finished. The gouged and eroded earth is sodden and the dun brown heritage is like wet moss. Sometimes a lonely stone cottage cringes forlorn beneath the leaden clouds.

This evocative description was written nearly forty years ago, since when Ashley's light-saturated paintings have become his trademark.

As the self-styled 'Yorkshire Artist', he has often said that what the Brontë sisters did with the pen, he wants to do with the brush – to capture the wild, ephemeral beauty of the moors. But in many ways his work bears closer similarity to that of another literary titan from Yorkshire, Ted Hughes. Just as Scout Rock overshadowed Hughes's childhood in Mytholmroyd so, too, did the Pennine moors around Barnsley with Ashley. Both men's work has been shaped by the Yorkshire landscape and shares the same primal thump. The birds scattered among Ashley's glowering skies are reminiscent of Hughes's black-backed gulls 'bent like an iron bar' as they are flung against the wind.

It is not difficult, either, to read poems like *Wind* and think of *Rain and Mist over Garsdale*, or *When all have gone home*, which captures the last shards of daylight as darkness descends to reclaim the land. As Hughes himself wrote in *Heptonstall*, 'Only the rain never tires'.

The Barnsley-born poet Ian McMillan believes Ashley's art captures a 'vision' of the Yorkshire landscape:

> He somehow gives it a melancholy feeling that's hard to describe and which is different from the man himself. When you meet him he's opinionated, he's jolly and full of energy and yet his work has a stillness and melancholy feel to it. I have a couple of his paintings and I never grow tired of them because there's depth in his work, it's not chocolate box stuff.

McMillan believes that his brand of populist art doesn't always garner the praise it deserves:

Modern art, in particular, can sometimes seem esoteric and hard to understand without having knowledge of art history, whereas Ashley's work is instantly accessible and a lot of people are very moved by his paintings. It's a bit like when I write a funny poem, it's not seen as artistically important as a serious poem and it's similar with Ashley's paintings. There's this view that if something is accessible and you 'get it' straight away, then somehow it's not as relevant, which I disagree with.

He admires, too, the fact that Ashley has remained in Yorkshire, keeping his muse close at hand:

There's a sense sometimes of prejudice against artists from the north and this idea that unless you're from London you won't be taken seriously. But part of his message is 'I'm from the north and I can do it' and it's as if he's waving two fingers at the art establishment. He's become himself, he's become Ashley Jackson the painter. He doesn't agree with the idea of subsidized art because he has always made his own living as an artist and I quite like that attitude.

In doing so he's become something of a Yorkshire treasure:

I noticed when I brushed past him once that he has incredibly strong muscles, which comes from gripping an easel all those years in the rain and wind, he's like Charles

Atlas. He reminds me, too, of Kirk Douglas when he plays Van Gogh in the film *Lust For Life*. Van Gogh used to love to be outside painting and it's the same with Ashley, he's like the Van Gogh of Kirklees.

The singer Tony Christie has known Ashley for more than thirty-five years, during which time he's built up a collection of his paintings:

We used to go over quite regularly with our kids who were around the same age as Claudia and Heather. I'd already bought one his paintings from his gallery in

Tony Christie with Ashley and Anne.

When all have gone home, Featherbed Moss.

Barnsley, but he had these two fantastic paintings on the wall in his house, which he thought were among his best ones. And one day after a few whiskys, because he's always very liberal with his drinks, I managed to get him to part with them, although I don't think Anne was very pleased.

The paintings in question were scenes of moorland fires that Ashley did during one of the long, hot summers during the mid-70s:

I think they're incredible works, you almost expect Heathcliff to emerge from the smoke. I've seen a lot of watercolours and most are just pencil sketches that have then been coloured in, but there's no pencil work in Ashley's paintings. Watercolours are often seen as the lower end of the art spectrum, but it takes a tremendous amount of skill to be good at painting them and there are few artists who can match Ashley.

Although their hectic schedules mean they rarely see each other these days, they remain good friends:

He's got this childlike innocence to him which is alien to his art, but that's part of his charm. I'd been living in Spain and we didn't see each other for twenty years, but we met up for a TV show with Richard Whiteley a while back. We had a few drinks afterwards and it was just like old times and he was the same lovable person.

Acclaimed sculptor Graham Ibbeson, who joined Ashley for

a UK exhibition in 2007, says he has helped him learn how to appreciate his own work:

We've helped each other out over the years and he's like a big brother to me. I've always been very critical of my own work but it was Ashley who taught me how to take a step back and value it, not in a financial sense, but to see it as other people do.

He believes that as a watercolourist, Ashley has few peers:

The job of an artist is to interpret their vision with an economy of style and he does this perfectly. When he's up on the moors he sees all its subtle changes, which he is somehow able to mirror with his brush.

He opens up his world to other people but he's only able to do that because of his deep love and respect of the Yorkshire landscape. He often calls it his church and every time he goes out to paint he's honouring nature.

There's been times I've heard people talking and they've looked up and said, 'I see it's an Ashley Jackson sky'. As an artist you can't get a better accolade than that. Not even Turner got that kind of reaction to his work.

What interests Ibbeson is the fact his paintings derive such power without ever containing any human figures:

As a sculptor my work is all about people, humour and social scenes. But Ashley's paintings have little or no reference to humanity in them and yet they can still move you. They are about more than just the landscape and a lot of people who might think they know his work don't fully appreciate how good he is. If you look at some of his recent landscapes they teeter on the verge of abstraction and I find these works incredible. They may look simple but there's a depth to them that few artists are able to create.

He believes that Ashley tells the 'truth' in his paintings:

He doesn't paint what he thinks people want to see, he paints what he sees and feels. Being an artist is a very lonely profession and he understands this. When he's up on the moors it's just himself and the landscape and that can be incredibly intense and I think his public persona is a release from this.

He likens his skill to that of another great Yorkshire artist:

Henry Moore could look at any object or surface and tell you its cubic capacity to within a couple of millimetres and Ashley has the same ability to read the landscape and understand light.

I remember a few years ago we were doing a photo shoot up on the moors and he looked at the sky and he told the photographer to wait five minutes because the wind was about to change and sure enough five minutes later it did and I swear to God, I looked up and it was an Ashley Jackson sky.

When the Wind Blows

# 19

# *Epilogue*

Since finishing *A Brush With Ashley* in 2001, the artist has been conspicuous by his absence from our TV screens. But at a time when most people of a pensionable age might be thinking about slowing down he continues to pound the countryside intent on perfecting his art. Even after more than half a century enduring everything a Pennine winter can throw at him, his enthusiasm remains undimmed, and he still runs his outdoor workshops, taking aspiring artists of all abilities out on to the moors above Holmfirth to teach them the intricacies of watercolour painting.

Although his TV appearances may be less frequent these days, his public persona hasn't diminished. In 2005 he was given the freedom of the City of London and the following year he won a Yorkshire Lifetime Achievement Award for his work promoting art and celebrating Yorkshire's landscape. In 2008, he joined such illustrious names as William Wilberforce, Fred Trueman and Dame Judi Dench in the Yorkshire Icon Awards' Hall of Fame.

His reputation as one of Britain's foremost watercolourists means he is still a big draw for galleries up and down the country. His 2008 exhibition, *Painting in the Open Air*, at the

Ashley's painting was used for the front cover of BT's phone book in 2003. This was quite an achievement as David Hockney is the only other artist to be recognized in this way.

Ashley meets American civil rights activist Jesse Jackson.

Laing Art Gallery, in Newcastle, included three sell-out painting demonstrations and more than 55,000 people visited the gallery during his three-month exhibition. In 2009 he became the first ever artist to have a copy of one of his paintings printed on a bank card, when he agreed to allow a painting of Langsett Moor to be used by the Yorkshire Bank to mark its 150th anniversary. It's a far cry from the days of the diffident schoolboy who first landed in Linthwaite all those years ago:

I was a Roman Catholic altar boy when I was a kid and from the age of fourteen I'd see the dead being brought in for a requiem and it hit me that I'd be there one day. And I told myself, 'If you want to be an artist, you have to get on your bike.'

But for all his flair and determination there was no guarantee he would succeed:

When I was younger my heart would be thumping as I was painting, because I didn't know if they were going to sell and I had a family to support. I haven't done commissions for a long time now, but in the early days if you wanted a portrait of your pet dog, I'd do it. I used to paint little Yorkshire terriers even though there were times when I felt like kicking them through the window because they were peeing on my studio floor. So I know what it's like to struggle.

Anyone who walks into his gallery today in Holmfirth – a stone's throw from Nora Batty's back porch – might find this hard to reconcile with the star-studded photos on display;

Ashley with Prince Charles, Ashley with his arm around a sparkling Sarah Ferguson, and Ashley with his old chums and fellow Yorkshire treasures Brian Glover and Bill Owen. Elsewhere, there's a picture of him with American civil rights activist Jesse Jackson and Bill Clinton accepting one of his original watercolours. But rather than being there to massage his ego, they are a reminder to him of the people he's met during what has been a remarkable journey:

What are the odds on someone with my background making a name for himself? They're not great. So when I look back at everything it seems unbelievable and I still

have to pinch myself sometimes. But I've had some great fun. I started out as a signwriter, I've taught prisoners how to paint, I've travelled to Europe, America and Asia and been invited to meet prime ministers, I mean what a life.

But while his gallery bears testament to a successful career, it hasn't come easily:

I've worked hard to get where I am today, there's no point me saying it was destiny, or it happened by chance. The best thing you can be blessed with is good health, but the rest is up to you.

This determination is a trait recognised by his daughter and manager, Claudia:

What is special about him is he has succeeded not only in following his own dream, but he's inspired others to follow theirs. Working with disadvantaged children has definitely been an eye opener and a reminder how different life could have been for dad.

His paintings have been his passport to a world that he wouldn't otherwise have seen. They have been exhibited all over the world and acquired by many famous people, from singers and writers, to politicians and princes. But while their patronage has undoubtedly helped his career he understands who his audience is:

It's not millionaires who usually come in and buy my originals, it's ordinary folk who want one of my paintings because it's their landscape, it's what they know and what they recognize.

Ashley with Paul Sykes in the Victoria Quarter, Leeds.

Ashley with the Duchess of York raising funds for the 'Children in Crisis Charity'.

He has painted some of the world's most dramatic landscapes; the Great Wall of China, the Sierra Nevada mountains of Andalusia and the American Rockies, but he finds nothing as compelling as the Pennine hills:

I'm nearly seventy and I'm still working, but I enjoy it, because I'm outside in mother nature's cathedral of the open air, I'm not working down a pit, or in a factory, that's hard graft – what I do is a privilege.

And his paintings, he says, are his legacy:

I can tell you where I was for each of them and what I was doing and every one tells a story. They're my memorial stones when I'm dead and gone.

Despite all the travelling he has done to exotic and far flung places he continues to live in Holmfirth. As well as having his gallery in the town he runs an art shop in Barnsley, where they've come to regard him as one of their own. But for all the plaudits his paintings have brought him there is one thing even more precious to him, his family – his two daughters, Heather and Claudia; his four grandchildren, Francesca, Meg, Oliver and Sam; and above all his wife Anne, who has been the rock upon which he's built his career.

Anne has always believed in me, even in the moments of despair when I've thought about throwing in the towel. She's the one who's taken care of the business side of things and she's the one who has the high blood pressure, not me. She gave me the freedom and confidence to paint. Without her I'd probably still be signwriting, so I owe her everything.

Like his idol Turner, Ashley's greatest gift is his mastery of light. Through the seemingly simple act of mixing paint and putting it on paper he is able to capture the spirit of a landscape that has entralled visitors for centuries. Marc Chagall once said that 'great art picks up where nature ends'. If that is true then Ashley Jackson is both an alchemist and mother nature's son.

Ashley and his grandchildren.

Ashley and his daughter and manager, Claudia.

# Index of Paintings